Bernie Sanders for President 2016

A Political Revolution

John Davis BA JD LLM

Bernie Sanders for President 2016:
A Political Revolution

John Davis, BA., J.D., LL.M.

Old Town Publishing

All rights reserved.

ISBN-13: **978-1515298809**

ISBN-10: **1515298809**

Kindle Edition

Library of Congress cataloguing in publication data available on request.

00-013243

10 9 8 7 6 5 4 3 2 1 2 3 4 5 6 7 8 9 10

DEDICATION

This book is dedicated to Senators Bernie Sanders and Elizabeth Warren, and all of those of us with modest beginnings who have devoted our lives to the enlightened service of the common man.

"I don't represent big corporations and I don't want
their money." Sen. Bernie Sanders

ACKNOWLEDGMENTS

The Author and Publisher would like to thank Senator Bernie Sanders. Throughout history, the vast majority of humanity has sought modest governance, and, the right to live peacefully and productively.

In moments of history, ruling classes emerged which sought self-gratification of greed, the quest for raw power, and the subjugation of the common man.

A few times in history, great men have come forward to challenge these tyrants, and, restore autonomy to the People in the name of peace, prosperity and the sanctity of human existence.

Bernie Sanders is such a man.

Table of Contents

BERNIE SANDERS FOR PRESIDENT 2016
A POLITICAL REVOLUTION

John Davis[1]

Introduction

This book is not just about Senator Bernie Sanders. It is about the people who support him. It is about a grass roots movement of Americans who share Senator Sanders' view of America. It is about the Americans who share Senator Sanders' vision for America. It is also about America itself.

The first part of the book is about the current problems in America and how they relate to our

---

[1] *Bacheloris Artis*, Case Western Reserve University 1975; *Juris Doctor*, Seattle University School of Law 1981; *Legis Magister*, New York University School of Law 1984.

history.

Unfortunately our current situation is dark. Many underestimate the challenges we, as a People, face in our current economic and political situation. Many also underestimate the dangers we face in the future if we do not change course. Although the first part of the book is dark, it is an accurate reflection of what Senator Sanders has, himself, noted in public appearances, and, in his many dissertations on what is needed for a just and prosperous American People.

The second part of the book is a comparison of our modern day problems with government, and, how they are related to the very same reasons our Founders revolted in the eighteenth century against the tyranny of the ruling class in Britain. The second part of the book goes through the reasons stated in the Declaration of Independence, for the American Revolution, and attempts to show that those same reasons exist, today, to support a political revolution against the ruling elite in the United States.

The third part of the book is a series of short chapters on Senator Sanders' platform. As Senator Sanders progresses in the election, his platform is evolving. However, this section of the book discusses 12 of the most prominent items on his agenda for reform, and revolution against the ruling elite in America. Most of Senator Sanders' agenda items are currently the subjects of legislation he is introducing in Congress, at present, to advance when he becomes President.

This book is a not a light-hearted treatment of just another political campaign of thousands in our history.

This book is an attempt to weave the solemn concepts of democracy, and the enlightenment of our Founders, into a context that illuminates their relevance to our modern day.

The author and publisher hope that it will empower the voters of the United States to comprehend the gravity of our current situation, and, empower supporters of Senator Sanders to argue effectively in favor of his platform.

PROLOGUE:
Situation Awareness

America, as we know it, no longer exists.

America was once both a dream, and a reality, based upon ancient principles of democracy, and, the dignity and sanctity of the individual. America, and Americans, were born from the brilliant insights of our Founders. Our Founders were men and women who had revived the ancient heroic concepts of humanity, and, who created a place in which the freedom, honor and prosperity of those men and women could endure. Our Founders foresaw the current dystopia and corruption that has taken hold of our country and its People. The question, in the upcoming elections in the U.S., is whether the safeguards of our Founders will prevail, or, whether the voting public will continue to be deceived, by corporate controlled propaganda, into perpetuating the Orwellian nightmare that has crept upon us.

The key candidate for President of the United

States is Senator Bernie Sanders of Vermont (I). On May 1, 2015, Senator Sanders announced his bid to seek the democratic nomination for President. Openly opposing the Democratic National Convention's [DNC] anointed candidate, Hillary Clinton, Senator Sanders (affectionately called "Bernie" in the Public eye) has declared himself a "candidate for the People."

Within twenty-four hours of announcing his candidacy, Bernie acquired over 200,000 volunteers, and over $1.5M in donations. Unlike Hillary Clinton and all of the republican candidates, Bernie's contributors were not large institutions, but were ordinary people, common people, who contributed an average of $30.00 each. Even more unique among Bernie's supporters was the fact that most of them had learned of Bernie's candidacy, not through the corporate controlled mainstream media (MSM), but through social networking and personal networking. By the middle of June 2015, he had raised $6,000,000 in small donations.

Bernie Sanders has become a "key" candidate in the upcoming election because he, and he alone, is raising concrete issues that have adversely affected Americans for roughly the past fifty years.

These issues can be summarized as being issues surrounding the realization that Americans are no longer being treated as equals, or even as humans entitled to human rights, by the institutions we created, empowered and trusted.

These issues (or problems) strike at the very heart of the American Dream.

Of all of the many candidates running for President in 2016, one candidate, and one candidate alone, Bernie Sanders, vows to support a platform that puts the needs of Americans above the schemes and designs of a ruling class.

Senator Sanders, alone, has a track record of representing the People of the United States, instead of the special interests that have come to dominate the government of the United States. Senator Sanders, alone, has a platform that will realistically restore the American Dream for hundreds of millions of Americans.

President Lincoln identified the American dream in his immortal Gettysburg Address. Unlike current politicians, lawyers and judges who are mainly ignorant of the basis for our laws and Constitution, President Lincoln knew the origins of the American dream.

Ancient Roman lawyers first identified that dream in the early periods of the first millennium. That dream, written in Latin, and eloquently translated by President Lincoln is:

"Omnes homines naturâ æquales sunt."

"All men are created equal."

And yet, all around us in American culture, we see vast inequalities between people, because of their birth, gender, social status, economic status and many other factors beyond their control.

These inequalities are being driven by a government, which has become so corrupt that it has become the principal oppressor of the people who empower it – the American voters. This corruption is not the result of American voters. It is a result of long-term corruption, and many inter-related workings of dishonest government officials, over a long period of time. Accompanying this corruption is the coordinated power of corporate controlled propaganda, and, the workings of corrupt journalists over that same period of time. The coordinated actions of a corrupt media, and a corrupt government, have resulted in a mass deception of Americans. This mass deception of Americans has led us to become the exact opposite of the nation our Founders envisioned.

This is not the first time in history this has happened to a great nation.

In the eighteenth century, in France, the French *philosophes*, a group of great thinkers who influenced our Founders, recognized that France had become a nation of tyranny and oppression under its monarchy. In the immortal words of one of those *philosophes*, Jean-Jacques Rousseau:

> *L'homme est né libre, et partout il est dans les fers, ...*

> "Man is born free, and yet everywhere he is in chains . . .."

No great quote from history could be more appropriate to the American people as we approach the presidential election in 2016.

Not only have Americans been enslaved by a corrupt government, and a corrupt corporate media, but also Americans have been fraudulently tasked to extending that enslavement, and corruption, beyond its own borders to the rest of the world.

What has been described as the *"Pax Ameri-cana"* (the world peace of America) is, in reality, a ruthless military machine, maintained at all costs to individuals in both the United States and in other countries, that is comprised of over 652 U.S. military bases, and which costs the U.S. taxpayers (almost exclusively middle class taxpayers) over one half of a Trillion dollars every year. The largest single item in this military budget is paying for military pensions. The entitlements are paid to former military officers who often go out and find high paying executive jobs in military-industrial complex. Once securing their job in the military industries in the U.S., and around the world, they use the influence of their friendships in the military to assure the continuations of massive arms purchases, and, massive arms sales to other nations. The average enlistee, who serves and is often disabled by military service, receives little of these gargantuan benefits, and, is often discharged into the general population with substantial physical, mental and social disabilities.

Notwithstanding our immense global military activity around the globe, America has become more and more dependent on foreign commodities that are under the control of large, multinational, corporations.

As ancient Rome was entirely dependent on grain from Egypt, our country has become entirely dependent upon hydrocarbon fuels from the Middle East and other areas of the world.

Our "American Dream," today, resembles the Roman Empire in about 40 B.C. (the time of Julius Caesar). We lay waste to vast areas of foreign countries, to provide wealth for only a few people, and yet our own people are going hungry, without medical care, and with no possibility of social or economic mobility.

That is not what our founders wanted. Our Founders, who were great scholars of antiquity, and ancient law, wanted a Republic that resembled the Roman Empire at its most peaceful and prosperous stages of development.

President Thomas Jefferson was a classics scholar. He spent most of his youth studying ancient Greek and Latin, and, studying the ancient political organizations in Greece and Rome. One of the books that inspired his design of the U.S. Constitution (and the declaration of Independence) was a book published in Germany known as "*Ius Gentium Methodo Scientifica Pertractatum*, by Christian Wolff.

The *"Ius Gentium,"* (sometimes spelled *"jus gentium"*) was the body of law ancient Rome, in its most peaceful and prosperous era, used to govern the many geographically, culturally and demographically diverse provinces of its empire.

President Lincoln eloquently translated the meaning of *"ius gentium"* in his timeless "Gettysburg Address:" "Government (or rule of law) of the people, by the people and for the people." The fundamental premise of the *ius gentium* was (and is): *"Omnes homines naturâ æquales sunt."* "All men are created equal."

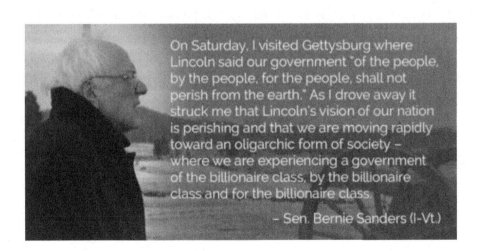

On Saturday, I visited Gettysburg where Lincoln said our government "of the people, by the people, for the people, shall not perish from the earth." As I drove away it struck me that Lincoln's vision of our nation is perishing and that we are moving rapidly toward an oligarchic form of society – where we are experiencing a government of the billionaire class, by the billionaire class and for the billionaire class.

– Sen. Bernie Sanders (I-Vt.)

The *ius gentium,* and its fundamental premise, under President Jefferson's brilliant design for our government, became the basis for, in President Lincoln's words: " . . . a new nation, conceived in liberty, and, dedicated to the proposition, "*Omnes homines naturâ æquales sunt.*" "All men are created equal."

Millions of soldiers in ancient Rome, went out into the world, fought and died for this principal. Many millions more, of the enemies of Rome, also died so that this principle would prevail. The same is true of the great experiment, America, and it soldiers and enemies. The most tragic of this confrontation over the premise, "all men are created equal," occurred in the great Civil War in which over 500,000 men died, on both sides, to promote the dream of equality between men.

Many people, in the wake of rampant revisionism, have lost sight of what the civil war was about. The Civil War did not begin as a war completely over slavery. Originally, President Lincoln in his first inaugural address promised that he would not interfere in the private ownership of slaves. The Confederate Constitution, adopted at secession, actually outlawed the international slave trade.

The Civil War began when Northern commercial groups corrupted the federal government to impose a tax that was aimed solely at crippling the economy of the South. The tax required Southerners, who were mostly dependent on agriculture, to pay heavy taxes on cotton they produced and other natural resources. During this period, less than 1.6% of Americans owned slaves. Slaves were mostly abused as agricultural workers (much like migrant Hispanic workers are abused today) to provide raw cotton for Eli Whitney's invention of the cotton gin. At the time, the cotton gin could process massive amounts of cotton, but there was, as yet, no machine for harvesting cotton from the fields.

U.S. slave-owners only indirectly drove slavery, in the U.S., to the point of the civil war. Foreign interests that profited heavily from the trans-oceanic trade in African slaves started most of the slavery in the U.S. Further, foreign banks, especially in the UK, profited heavily from financing the international slave trade, and from mortgages and security interests they held in Southern plantations.

Slavery was legal in the U.S., not just because of a few Southern slave-owners, but, because slavery had been legal, under the U.S.

Constitution and the American flag, for over 88 years before President Lincoln's Emancipation Proclamation (freeing all slaves). A reading of Carl Sandburg's work on Abraham Lincoln shows that even President Lincoln "freed the slaves" reluctantly, and, mostly to obtain the financial support of abolitionists in Congress.

The Civil War, and the incredibly brave men who fought on both sides, began the awareness, among Americans, that government could be corrupted to control economic power in a way that enslaved people economically, as well as through legal status as it had enslaved African-Americans. A government which corrupts economic power is one that renders men unequal, and, places them in chains. It renders men unequal by giving certain classes of persons certain economic privileges under the disguise of "legitimate government interests." The fact is, that there is no end or limit to "legitimate government interests." Consequently, there is no end or limit to which corrupt politicians and special interests can justify corruption in the name of "legitimate government interests."

How is this corruption possible? The corruption is possible because of various legal superstitions invented by corrupt and incompetent judges.

At one time in our history we had an educated judiciary comprised of judges who fully understood the concepts of freedom, liberty, individuality (or non-conformity) . . . and all other philosophical notions that underlie the concepts of equality between people. Competent judges viewed our Constitution as a document that did not grant absolute power to government. Competent judges, at the time of the formation of our country, viewed the U.S. Constitution as a document that limits our government's power.

Todays corrupt and incompetent judges, mindless of the origins of the Constitution, and the millions of common men who died defending it, view the Constitution as a document, which places absolute and unlimited power in government and the people in control of government. In the words of one of the most corrupt and incompetent judges of our time, William Rehnquist: "We will establish law and order no matter what the cost to individual liberties." "Law and Order" (known to the Nazi's as: "*Recht und Ordnung*"), when it comes at the expense of ANY individual liberties, is what we know as the definition of fascism. Legal scholars have, euphemistically, labeled this fascism "social control."[2]

Fascism is a very efficient form of government. Under fascism, the government owns or controls everything. Under fascism, individuals cannot do anything unless it is "permitted" by the government. Under fascism, the government has no responsibility; it has only power over people. Under fascism, the people have no rights, they have only responsibilities to the government, and those favored by the government. (Sound familiar?)

America's education system has deteriorated, significantly, over the last half of a century. America's education system is so obsessed with political correctness, and providing workers for large corporations (notwithstanding the fact that very few college graduates ever find gainful employment), that our education system is incapable of providing students with critical thinking skills, or, objective analysis skills.

The result is that America now has several generations of "educated" [perhaps "indoctrinated"] voters who are completely unable to distinguish between legitimate legal and political is-

---

[2] McCall, Madhavi M. and McCall, Michael A., *Chief Justice Wiliam Rehnquist: His Law-and-Order Legacy and Impact on Criminal Justice*, 39 AKRON LAW R. 323, (2006).

sues, and "political correctness." The mass media has contributed enormously to the dumbing down of America. The "dumbing down" of America, along with obesity (from processed foods), is now a widespread international joke. Americans are now seen, worldwide, as "fat and stupid."

Let's look at the Civil War as an example of America "dumbing down" in favor of political correctness.

Public schools, universities, and the mass media have combined to convince the public, successfully, that all Southerners were evil slavers and that the Civil War was only about slavery. This political correctness arose out of the one-sided media coverage of the civil rights movement in the 1960's and 1970's, and subsequent revisions to history. Fortunately, the civil rights movement succeeded to a large extent, racial violence has abated, and racism, as a whole, although it unfortunately survives on the margins, is no longer a mainstream ideology.

Nevertheless, a historian trying to point out the fact that the Civil War was not only about slavery is likely to be branded a "racist," "bigot," "liar," "white supremacist," "race baiter," "KKK sympathizer," and a virtually unlimited litany of other politically correct insults.

It is important to study the Civil War, with accuracy, and, without the perversions of modern political correctness, because many of the factors that lead to the South's seccession, and the war itself, are present in today's corrupt federal and state governments.

The South traded extensively with the UK, and Europe, while the South was developing as an economic region.   Through its open water ports in Savannah and its network of railways, from Savannah to various points in the South, Southerners had been able to maintain a certain amount of economic independence from the North.   When Eli Whitney created the steam-powered cotton gin in England, it was a tremendous boost to the agricultural export capabilities of the South.   Northern industrialists, however, had little to sell to European nations in order to enhance the wealth of the already wealthy Northern industrialists.

The result is that wealthy Northern industrialists openly bribed the entire Congress of the U.S. to impose a 40% tax on any goods that the South produced (to cripple the ability of Southern cotton growers to earn a profit or trade cotton overseas). At the same time, Congress had also been bribed to impose a 50% tax on any items that the South imported from Europe. The result of this corruption (under color of law) was that the wealthy Northern industrialists would be able to buy the South's agricultural products and natural resources at ten cents on the dollar.

Even more oppressive to the South, the wealthy Northern industrialists continued their campaign against the South, during and after the war. Sherman's "March to the Sea" was not so much a direct strategic military objective. In his "March to the Sea" northern General Sherman completely destroyed all of the rail lines tying Atlanta and the South to the port of Savannah. This would insure that, after the war was over, the South would be required to trade with the wealthy Northern industrialists, rather than have alternative trade arrangements with Europe.

Sherman's "March to the Sea" was not an open confrontation between troops. It was "total warfare" waged against an un-defended civilian population. Sherman himself acknowledged that he could do more damage to civilians in the

South by simply moving his Army, in a scorched earth policy, in a way that brought famine and disease upon the civilians in the South as punishment for secession. Sherman's "March to the Sea" was a war crime that, to this day, has helped perpetuate racism in the South.

Why is this important to the election in 2016? It is important because wealthy owners of multi-national corporations have done the exact same thing to the American people as the North did to the South. This time, the aggression and greed of the wealthy is not directed against just a geographic area, such as the South, it is directed against the entire middle class. The wealthy, in this war against the People, have employed a corruption of governmental power that far exceeds what was applied against Americans during the Civil War.

In the past fifty years, economic powers, both foreign and domestic, have destroyed millions of Americans, and destroyed the American dream itself. What was once a dream of individual freedom has, under various pretenses, become a dystopian and Orwellian ordeal for most Americans.

How did this happen, and, what caused it?

What happened is that we, as Americans, have developed a paradigm, which completely dehumanizes the American people. Americans, pitted against each other by social issues, are obsessed with blame and hatred of other Americans. Americans are relentlessly pursuing rationalizations and justifications for blaming, hating, and punishing other Americans. Punishment of Americans, at the hands of government, has become the sole waking objective of the corporate controlled media, and the corporate controlled government.

As President Lincoln so eloquently reaffirmed: "A house divided against itself, cannot stand." Americans are now more divided than ever, and, in those endless distractions of blame and punishment, have yielded full control over our nation to the special interests that control our punishing government. We no longer live among neighbors and friends . . . we live among servants of a state that considers its own people "the enemy."

The cause of this mass dehumanization is a media, and a government, that know no boundaries, and, which are completely out of control.

Our founders anticipated this happening, and, they provided safeguards in our Constitution to correct and reverse the fascism that is currently in possession of our country. Unfortunately, however, our Founders never anticipated that the judges in the United States would, as a group, treasonously refuse to enforce the Constitution.

The word "treasonous" is appropriate in describing the situation. When judges assume office, they are pledged to uphold the Constitution of the United States. That oath has become meaningless in the past seventy years because judges have, without any authority from the Constitution, given themselves the power to define the Constitution, as they please, instead of in the manner in which the Founders intended. Today's judges are "willfully blind" to the fact that they interpret the Constitution as a document that gives the federal and state governments unlimited power, and, at the same time, takes all power away from American men, women and children.

The Constitution was never intended to give unlimited power to the federal or state governments. It was intended to limit the power of federal and state governments, and, convey protected power to the American people, as individuals, in all matters.

This transition to a post-constitutional country did not happen overnight in America, and did not arise from a single cause. It occurred over time, carefully disguised by the mass media, and represents a repeat of the same historical circumstances that lead to the formation of the United States in the first place.

To quote the great trial lawyer, Clarence Darrow: "History repeats itself . . . that's one of the things wrong with history."

The Causes for Revolution:
The Ruling Elite as King George

Since the Wall Street crash of 2008, more than 99% of all new income has gone to the top 1%.

America needs a political revolution.

BERNIESANDERS.COM

We can identify what is wrong with America today by looking no further that President Jefferson's Declaration of Independence. President Jefferson's exact wording does not directly apply to what Americans, today, are suffering at the hands of their corrupted government. (A government corrupted by wealthy individuals and multinational corporations). However, we can take President Jefferson's characterization of the abuses of King George, in England, and show how our own corrupt government, today, is oppressing the American people just as King George abused the colonials.

The means that King George, in England, used to oppress the American people in 1776, are the same means of oppression being used by our corrupt governments, today, to serve multinational corporations and wealthy interests. In reading the Declaration of Independence as relative to today's oppressors of the common man, simply substitute the references in the Declaration to King George with the concept of the "ruling class" in 21st Century America.

The Declaration of Independence begins as follows:

IN CONGRESS, July 4, 1776.

The unanimous Declaration of the thirteen united States of America,

When in the Course of human events,
it becomes necessary for one people to
dissolve the political bands which have

connected them with another, and to assume among the powers of the earth, the separate and equal station to which the Laws of Nature and of Nature's God entitle them, a decent respect to the opinions of mankind requires that they should declare the causes which impel them to the separation.

We hold these truths to be self-evident, that all men are created equal, that they are endowed by their Creator with certain unalienable Rights, that among these are Life, Liberty and the pursuit of Happiness.--That to secure these rights, Governments are instituted among Men, deriving their just powers from the consent of the governed, --That whenever any Form of Government becomes destructive of these ends, it is the Right of the People to alter or to abolish it, and to institute new Government, laying its foundation on such principles and organizing its powers in such form, as to them shall seem most likely to effect their Safety and Happiness.

. . .

Such has been the patient sufferance of these Colonies; and such is now the necessity, which constrains them to alter their former Systems of Government. The history of the present King of Great Britain is a history of repeated injuries and usurpations, all having in direct object the establishment of an absolute Tyranny over these States. To prove this, let Facts be submitted to a candid world.

President Jefferson then enumerates the bases that Colonial Americans had for seceding from the rule of King George and his supporters ("the ruling class.")

Let's examine each of these points of oppression that President Jefferson enumerated in the Declaration of Independence. We'll first explore what each of these points meant in the context of 18th Century America, and, how the same oppression is being used by our own corrupt government, today, against the American People.

Todays Declaration of Independence

I. HE HAS REFUSED HIS ASSENT TO LAWS, THE MOST WHOLESOME AND NECESSARY FOR THE PUBLIC GOOD.

This point of contention in the Declaration of Independence referred to the fact that King

George had the authority to veto any laws that Americans wanted for their governance.

For example, President Jefferson, and the Founding Fathers, arranged to have laws passed to abolish slavery. King George, however, vetoed that law because slavery was very profitable for the English government, and multinational businesses in England. King George wanted the slave trade to the U.S., and the profits of the British slave trade, to continue to engorge the British treasury and appease some of the greed of wealthy British interests. In addition, British bankers owned mortgages on all of the plantations. They also profited, immensely, from not allowing Americans to abolish slavery at the time of Independence because they held security interests in slaves.

Is there something similar to slavery in today's America?

To quote President John Adams: "There are two ways to conquer and enslave a country. One is by the sword. The other is by debt."

It is difficult to describe to current generations how a system, into which they have been born and raised, is a nefarious infraction on their freedom. America's current system of debt is as binding on human freedoms and dignity as the institution of slavery itself. Most Americans, thinking they are "free" have no idea how many economic special interests are combining to enslave each individual for his or her entire life. As Harriet Tubman, the famous African-American abolitionist said: "I freed a thousand slaves. I could have freed a thousand more if only they knew they were slaves."

President John F. Kennedy tried to warn the People of the United States that the power of the Federal Reserve Bank was a step toward enslaving the American People with debt. Seven days before he was assassinated he made the following comment: "There's a plot in this country to enslave every man, woman and child. Before I leave this high and noble office, I intend to expose this plot." In today's world, we are so used to ignoring the inflated rhetoric of politicians that we overlook the possibility that President Kennedy's words should be taken literally. However, there have been so many laws passed, in recent decades, that can only be described as "gifts" to banks and lending institutions, at the expense of the ordinary workers in America, that our current legal system can only be described as completely enslaving the American people through debt. This is accomplished through the almost unlimited economic power of the private Federal Reserve Bank in the U.S.

President Jefferson warned us about the dangers of a central bank, such as the Federal Reserve Bank. Throughout history such banks have been used to enslave more people than violence. President Jefferson wrote:

> *If the American people ever allow private banks to control the issue of their currency, first by inflation, then by deflation, the banks and corporations that will grow up around them will deprive the people of all property until their children wake up homeless on the continent their Fathers conquered...I believe that banking institutions are more dangerous to our liberties than standing armies... The issuing power should be taken from the banks and restored to the people, to whom it properly belongs.*

Despite what President Jefferson gave us in the way of enlightened caution, the American People are barely waking up to the fact that 20% or more of our children live in poverty, that we have 600,000 homeless people, that multinational corporations completely control our food, transportation, communications and housing infra-structures, and that fewer and fewer

Americans are able to make even a minimal standard of living.

The abuse of debt, by banks, multi-national corporations, and the government itself is at the root of almost all of our current economic and social problems.

Debt, itself, is arguably a necessary, or at least constructive, component of modern society. If properly regulated and contained, the system of debt for the ordinary person, that exists in this country, could be viewed as being benign. The problem is that our system of debt is not regulated. There is only a pretense of regulating debt in this country. The system of debt in this country is overseen by "captive agencies" (government entities which are corruptly controlled by the lenders) so that there is, literally, no possibility that common borrowers will have ANY ability to meaningfully negotiate the terms of their debt. Willingly complicit in this scheme to enslave, through debt, is a vast system of judges who have no intention of ever following any laws that are passed to place limitations on lenders, or, protect consumers from abusive lending practices. Under our current corrupt and incompetent judiciary's attitudes, banks are entitled to equal protection of the laws - Americans are not entitled to equal protection of the laws – the banks must always prevail.

During America's golden years in the 1950's, it was not uncommon for Americans to be debt-free except for a modest mortgage (at interest rates of 2-4%) or a modest car loan (at similarly modest interest rates).

Today, however, there is a deliberate and concerted effort to encumber everyone, with as much debt as possible, as soon as possible in their lives. In many ways it is a class war, in which the poor and middle class are targeted. The poor and middle class, because of low wages, high debt, high interest payments, and price gouging by large corporations, utilities and institutions, such as colleges and universities, have no choice but to go into debt in order to have any hope of participating in the world economy.

Additionally, the poor and middle class do not have safety nets for taking risks, unlike upper class persons. The poor cannot afford any economic risks. If a poor person takes an improvident economic risk in our economy, he may very well lose the ability to provide the basic necessities of food and housing for himself and his family. Consequently, the poor and middle class are constrained to paying massive debts that they have no choice but to contract. They have to pay these debts, even if not legally obligated to do so, because of a system of corrupt "credit reporting."

The national "credit reporting" system is a sham. It has one purpose, one purpose only . . . that purpose is to allow the wealthy, the banks and the creditors to get around the court system and deny the poor and the middle class any access to the courts, and any protection of the laws, on issues of consumer debt.

Under the system of "credit reports" currently in the U.S., a creditor can ruin the credit rating of anyone simply by reporting that they are displeased with their relationship with the person who borrowed money from them, or bought something from them. The bank or other creditor is not required to provide any proof other than their claim that they are displeased over a person's performance on debt or contractual terms. The result is that if you have a dispute with a creditor, the creditor doesn't have to spend the money to go to court and prove their claim. The creditor doesn't have to go to court to give you a chance to defend yourself, or assert your rights under the laws. The creditor can ruin your ability to get loans, jobs, advancements of all sorts, etc., simply by claiming that you are a "deadbeat."

Theoretically, there are laws in place which protect you from abuses of the credit reporting system. However, as any competent trial lawyer knows, the costs of suing a credit reporting company, such as Experian, and the bank or other creditor that made a false report against you, is about $150,000 in attorney's fees and costs. No person who is struggling to feed their family, and, meet the financial demands of everyday life, has that kind of money to seek justice. Consequently, those in the middle class and the poor are, literally, the slaves of those who control the credit reporting system.

II. HE HAS FORBIDDEN HIS GOVERNORS TO PASS LAWS OF IMMEDIATE AND PRESSING IMPORTANCE, UNLESS SUSPENDED IN THEIR OPERATION TILL HIS ASSENT SHOULD BE OBTAINED; AND WHEN SO SUSPENDED, HE HAS UTTERLY NEGLECTED TO ATTEND TO THEM.

One of the important aspects of the U.S. which Mr. Sanders has exposed in his campaign, is that it is virtually impossible to pass any law in the U.S. without the approval of Corporate America.

Most people in the U.S., unless they have been involved in the deep inner recesses of Wall

Street, usually cannot understand (or believe) how it is possible to corrupt the entire U.S. government.

When the ordinary voter thinks of "corruption," they have an image of large amounts of $100.00 bills changing hands, in dark chambers, within the recesses and shadows of the Capitol building or the Whitehouse.

There are, however, millions of ways to "buy" senators and representatives without cash or money ever changing hands directly.

One of the most popular (and legal) ways that senators and representatives, and presidents are bought off in the U.S. is through the exchange of expensive "favors."

Super Pacs, for example, are permitted under Supreme Court rulings (the Citizen's United case) to raise hundreds of millions of dollars, and, spend them on getting politicians elected to office. [A "PAC" is a "Political Action Committee" which is essentially free of any election contribution constraints]. Only a fool would think that this amount of money would be spent on a candidate without the insiders for the PAC expecting favors in return from the politician who is ultimately elected to office.

Further, it is not necessary for Wall Street, or major corporations, to "buy off" all of the members of Congress in order to control Congress.

This can be difficult for most people to understand, but, it is only necessary for large corporations to control 15-17% of the members of Congress, through massive PAC campaign contributions, in order to control the entire Congress.

The reason that corrupters need to "own" only 15%-17% of Congress, in order to control the American people, is that on any given law, or issue proposed in Congress, there is always likely to be a natural division among members of Congress. This is especially true in our two-party system. On any gun control issue, for example, half of the members of Congress will likely vote **against** the issue (no matter what it is), and, the other half of Congress is likely to vote **for** the measure. Consequently, all that is necessary to insure that the measure is either defeated or passed is to control the "swing vote."

In very simple terms, no law will ever pass if only 50% of Congress will vote for it.

In reality, few issues or laws are ever split

evenly down the middle at 50%. Almost all proposed laws and issues, however, will have roughly 50% supporters (+/- 15-17%), and, will have roughly 50% detractors (+/- 15-17%). The ancients understood this fact of human nature when they created the concept of the "supermajority," or the 2/3-majority vote.

A 2/3-majority vote (50% + 15-17%), in Congress, is required to override a Presidential veto. In addition, even if 65% of the representatives and senators, in Congress, oppose a particular bill, and only 35% of the voting members of Congress will support it, by controlling 15-17% of the vote, it is possible to still get the bill passed by a 51% majority of the vote in Congress.

When our Founders designed our government, they drew upon centuries of experience from philosophers and political scientists in Europe and the United Kingdom. One of the features they designed into our system was a very large House of Representatives (currently with 435 members). Theoretically, it would be very hard to bribe all 435 members. However, with control of the swing vote, it is only necessary to bribe 15-17% of those members, or 66 members of the House of Representatives, in order to control most or all of the votes and legislation in the

House of Representatives.

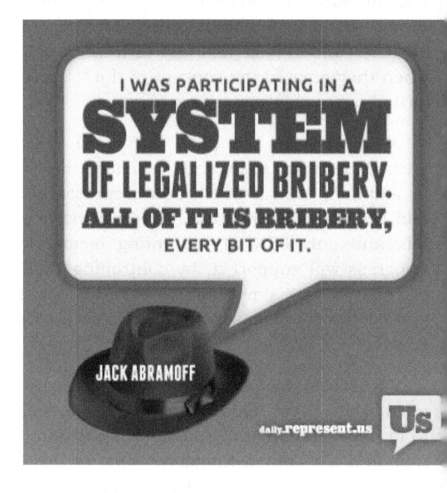

In terms of bribing the Senate, even less senators than representatives need to be bribed in order to acquire the swing vote. Therefore, to control all of the legislation in the Senate, it is only necessary to bribe 15-17 senators in order to control the vote on most issues.

What Senator Sanders and his supporters have shown is that it is relatively easy to bribe senators and representatives with relatively small amounts of money (from $10,000 to a few million). If that sounds like a lot of money . . .. it is not a lot of money compared to how much money special interests gain from corrupting our government. It is not a lot of money at all when one considers how much money is at stake in most of the laws that are passed in Congress.

The secretive passage of the Trans Pacific Partnership Agreement, for example, is worth, literally, trillions of dollars to the interests that have bribed the senators and representatives to assure that it is passed. Those special interests are prepared to spend Billions of dollars for its passage so that they can export U.S. jobs to slave labor countries, yet still extract hundreds of Billions from Americans for cheap imported goods.

III. HE HAS REFUSED TO PASS OTHER
      LAWS FOR THE ACCOMMODATION OF
      LARGE DISTRICTS OF PEOPLE, UNLESS

THOSE PEOPLE WOULD RELINQUISH THE RIGHT OF REPRESENTATION IN THE LEGISLATURE, A RIGHT INESTIMABLE TO THEM AND FORMIDABLE TO TYRANTS ONLY.

This reason for the Declaration of Independence revolved around King George doing everything possible to disempower local councils and governments in the Colonies. The King feared that popular assemblies in America were growing too large and powerful, as new communities were formed, and, as new representatives were elected to the assemblies of the colonies. Self-governance of the Colonials threatened the absolute power of the ruling class in England.

As a tyrant over Colonial America, King George had the power to deny the ordinary people from assembling, and passing, laws that governed the Colonies on local issues. The King did not want the people to have representation on local issues because the King wanted absolute control over every economic and political aspect of the life of Colonials.

This same condition exists, today, in America, with a corrupt Congress, and corrupt courts, controlled by the ruling class (1%), which routinely deny the right of self-governance to the people directly on the local level.

Congress has accomplished this tyranny by perverting two very important aspects of the Constitution. The judges on the U. S. Supreme Court invented the perversion.

The first Constitutional provision to be perverted is what is known as "The Supremacy Clause" in the U.S. Constitution.[3] The Supremacy clause essentially provides that in the event there is a conflict between federal laws, and state laws, then the federal laws control over the state laws.

This is a sound provision of the Constitution necessary for sound government. This provision is necessary for the federal government to perform its principal function of assuring harmonious relations between states having widely diverse geographic, demographic, political and religious characteristics.

However, at the time that the Founders designed the Constitution, the U. S. Constitution

---

[3] Article VI, Clause 2 U. S. Constitution

was viewed as a limitation on government power. As America's government became more and more wealthy, and more and more powerful in the 20th Century, so many corrupting influences have successfully gained control of the federal government, that the U. S. Constitution is now viewed by the 1%, and the judges and politicians they control, as an enabling document. The ruling class now enforces the Constitution as a document that grants unlimited government powers over the people in order to carry out the corrupt agendas of the ruling class. This was exactly the opposite of what our Founders intended.

Our Founders intended that the federal government would serve the states, and the people, instead of the other way around.

Here is an example of how perverted the Constitution's supremacy clause has become.

Vermont, coincidentally the home state of Senator Sanders, recently passed legislation requiring food manufacturers to indicate on packaging if any of their food contains Genetically Modified Organisms [GMOs]. Most informed consumers do not want to consume GMOs because they are linked to many illnesses, and, tend to allow accumulations of poisons in the food. When people consume food with GMOs, over time, they are likely to also accumulate the toxins in their tissues and organs. It could be centuries before scientists determine the full extent of the influence of GMOs on human civilization. As a result many consumers may choose not to purchase GMOs in favor of organic foods, or, foods that are not derived from genetically modified organisms.

Within weeks of Vermont being the first state to require GMO labeling, Monsanto Corporation, the American food giant, had influenced a small group of representatives in Congress to introduce a law that would prohibit the states from passing laws which required GMO labeling. The law, House Resolution 1599, also known as the "Dark Act," would allow large food processing and food manufacturing companies to deceive consumers by labeling GMO based foods as "all-natural."

I BELIEVE THAT WHEN A MOTHER GOES TO THE STORE AND PURCHASES FOOD FOR HER CHILD, SHE HAS THE RIGHT TO KNOW WHAT SHE IS FEEDING HER CHILD.

- Sen. Bernie Sanders

This is exactly the same kind of tyranny that the King of England imposed on colonials, depriving them of the right of local laws they passed for their own protection, if those laws in anyway interfered with the greed and deceit of the King and his friends.

IV. HE HAS CALLED TOGETHER LEGISLATIVE BODIES AT PLACES UNUSUAL, UNCOMFORTABLE, AND DISTANT

FROM THE DEPOSITORY OF THEIR PUBLIC RECORDS, FOR THE SOLE PURPOSE OF FATIGUING THEM INTO COMPLIANCE WITH HIS MEASURES

This abuse by the King, against colonial America, is echoed in modern government. King George did everything possible to make it impossible for colonials to participate in the making of laws in colonial America. He did this by convening legislative conventions in only two places – Boston and Virginia.

In Colonial America, it took days or weeks to travel to locations on horseback. In addition, there was no efficient or cost-effective means of transmitting documents and records over long-distances (as there is today). There were no fax machines, Internet or telephones. If someone wanted information from documents, they had to go to the geographic location where the documents were stored or archived. Consequently, people wanting to participate in legislative conventions, because of the King's orders, were unable to make informed decisions so that they could meaningfully participate in the government's process of making laws.

We do not need to look very far in modern

America to see how our own government uses this same tool of oppression against the people.

For example, President Obama, and key legislators who are under the intense influence of big money interests, recently proposed "fast track authority" for the President to negotiate a treaty, with Pacific Basin interests, known as the "Trans-Pacific Partnership" Agreement, or "TPP" for short.

In order to prohibit the American people from knowing anything about this international treaty, before Congress is to vote on it, President Obama, the Congress, and others under the control of large business and money interests, ordered that the contents of the agreement be kept secret from the public.

A copy of the agreement was available for senators and representatives to view, in the Capitol building, but nowhere else. Our elected leaders were not permitted to make copies of the agreement for fear that the People of the United States might learn the content of the proposed Agreements. Our representatives were not even permitted to make notes on the agreement.

One of the consequences of depriving voters

of information about this agreement, before laws are passed with respect to it, is that the agreement is really a thinly disguised form of corporate welfare. We know from some members of Congress who enlightened us, that the agreement provides almost unlimited power to multinational corporations to take money out of the U.S. economy, and invest the money overseas, solely for their own profits. Those who move American jobs, and American capital, to other countries, under the agreement, have no obligations to the People of the Untied States. Those who move the jobs and capital are not required to pay back taxes to the U.S. for the infrastructure they used to generate the money. They are not required to compensate the U.S. for the jobs they terminated. The agreement also has a method of absolving multinational corporations from responsibilities to laws in the U.S. In addition, it provides numerous mechanisms for circumventing U.S. laws designed to protect U.S. citizens.

The TPP provides for an alternate system of courts that are superior to the U.S. Government and courts established to protect the People of the United States.

The rules for these alternate courts provide that their decisions take precedence over laws passed by the United States government and its local states. No one may have access to these courts except the United States government and big businesses. If ordinary people need access to these almighty international business courts, the only way they can access the courts is if the United States is willing to go to court for those people. Because of the expense (to the taxpayers) of going to these international tribunals, it is not likely that the U.S. would ever agree to represent individuals or small groups of people, or small businesses in these courts.

V. HE HAS DISSOLVED REPRESENTATIVE HOUSES REPEATEDLY, FOR OPPOSING WITH MANLY FIRMNESS HIS INVASIONS ON THE RIGHTS OF THE PEOPLE.

This reason for revolution, as stated in the Declaration of Independence, is a little more difficult to relate to modern times.

Our Founders intentionally constructed our Constitution to prohibit anyone from dissolving the governments of states, cities and counties. This aspect of the Constitution was, in part, intended to address the abuses of King George. If a local government in colonial America criticized the King, the King would simply dissolve that Colonial branch of government as retaliation.

The federal government, in our modern times, doesn't directly dissolve local governments. Instead, the U.S. Supreme Court has created a doctrine known as the "pre-emption doctrine." The Supreme Court reserves the power to the U.S. Government to dissolve the power of states, counties and cities, on specific issues.

This is a sensible doctrine of law if used sparingly. In the event Congress wants, or needs, full control over a specific area of American, culture, the economy, politics or other areas, Congress can effectively make certain that no local governments pass laws that contradict Congress.

The modern problems with the pre-emption doctrine do not arise from the concept of pre-emption, and federal supremacy, in passing laws. The problems arise from corrupt and incompetent federal judges who dissolve local laws, by whimsically stretching the application of the pre-emption doctrine, to invalidate local laws the doctrine was never intended to invalidate.

Let's take a modern example.

Monsanto (which effectively owns various branches of government through its corrupting influence)[4] is an international food giant. Solely to increase its profits, it routinely engages in genetic engineering of crops and seeds [creating Genetically Modified Organisms or "GMOs"]. They routinely use experimental farms in Hawaii, to grow experimental GMOs, because Hawaii has a long, warm and moist growing season. The GMO experimentation by Monsanto does not necessarily cause problems for local farmers in Hawaii unless the GMO plants escape Monsanto's farms, and, seed the lots of other farmers. This happens usually when animals carry seeds to non-GMO farms, or, the

---

[4] Four of the five justices on the U.S. Supreme Court are former attorneys for Monsanto, and, have ruled in favor of Monsanto in virtually every case that has been brought before the Court. The head of the U. S. Food and Drug Administration is the former Vice President for Monsanto.

wind carries seeds to non-GMO farms. If that happens, then, local farmers have very serious problems, because of the GMO's growing in their farms, without the knowledge or permission of the local farmers.

The problem with GMO's is that they tend to (a) decimate the population of pollinators (especially honey bees which are the most efficient); (b) they tend to corrupt the genetic material in adjacent non GMO fields of crops; (c) they tend to make weeds resistant to herbicides because of Monsanto using glyphosates (Roundup™[5] weed killer) in the testing; and (d) GMO's have a high probability, under objective scientific studies, of creating numerous links to human illness and disease, as well as contamination of the DNA pool in wildlife, insects and fish.

To address these risks and hazards, Maui (County of Maui) passed a resolution that imposed a moratorium on GMO's being grown in Maui until such time as reliable scientific studies establish their safety.

Monsanto and its minions filed suit against the County, in federal court, claiming that the

---

[5] Monsanto owns the trademark for Roundup.

County had no authority to protect its citizens. Their reasoning was that Congress had already taken full authority to protect the citizens of the U.S. from safety hazards of growing experimental crops (and weeds).

A federal judge, not surprisingly, agreed with Monsanto and its affiliates. The judge overturned the local law on the grounds that the "Federal Plant Protection Act"[6] precluded anyone but the federal government from doing anything about dangerous or noxious plants in the U.S.

On reading the opinion, one can only conclude that the judge in question had no intention of looking at the case in any other way but to find in favor of the rich and powerful Monsanto (and its rich and powerful attorneys). The corruption in the U.S., among judges, has become so commonplace that we have assigned a euphemism to it. We call it "judicial activism." Loosely defined "judicial activism" is when a judge just makes up their own laws because they don't like the laws that Congress has written.

---

[6] (Pub. L. 106–224, title IV, §402, June 20, 2000, 114 Stat. 438.) (2000)

In this case, the judge decided that by Congress authorizing the Food and Drug Administration to pass regulations regarding the transportation of weeds across state lines, that Congress intended to remove all powers from state and local governments to do anything about weeds.

The general public might think that such rulings would be overturned by a court of appeals. However, the appellate court system in the U.S. is just as corrupt, or more corrupt, that our systems of trial courts. There is very little chance that an appellate court will reverse the poor decisions of trial courts unless the attorneys for the losing party have a heavy influence over the appellate court judges. There are a few exceptions to this general tactic by appellate courts, but those exceptions are so rare they are not worth mentioning.

This omnipresent corruption in our court system arose, primarily, because of the incredibly poor legal education system in the U.S. during the 1980's to the present. A thorough explanation of this phenomenon is beyond the scope of this introduction. However, it is safe to say that since law students are no longer required to study reasoning, the scientific method or Aristotelian logic, that our court system in the U.S. has become nothing more than a franchise of petty tyrants who consider themselves, and other judges, to be completely above the law.[7]

99% of the time, this corruption of kangaroo courts works against the individual people in our society, and in favor of large and powerful institutions.

In the words of an esteemed federal Judge, Hon. Edith Jones of the U.S. Court of Appeals for the Fifth Circuit: "The American legal system has been corrupted almost beyond recognition."[8]

---

[7]   See, Pahis, Stratos, CORRUPTION IN OUR COURTS: WHAT IT LOOKS LIKE AND WHERE IT IS HIDDEn, 118 Yale L.J. 1900 (2009). ("**Abstract**. Recent surveys and events indicate that judicial corruption could be a significant problem in the United States. This Note builds an economic model of bribery to better understand the incentives behind this pernicious phenomenon. It then compiles a data set of discovered incidents of judicial bribery in the United States to test the effectiveness of our anti-judicial-corruption institutions. This analysis suggests that our institutions are particularly ineffective at preventing and uncovering judicial bribery in civil disputes and traffic hearings.

[8] Hawkins, Geraldine, *"American Legal System is Corrupt Beyond Recognition, Judge Tells Harvard Law School,"* MassNews.com (2003).

VI. HE HAS REFUSED FOR A LONG TIME, AFTER SUCH DISSOLUTIONS, TO CAUSE OTHERS TO BE ELECTED; WHEREBY THE LEGISLATIVE POWERS, INCAPABLE OF ANNIHILATION, HAVE RETURNED TO THE PEOPLE AT LARGE FOR THEIR EXERCISE; THE STATE REMAINING IN THE MEAN TIME EXPOSED TO ALL THE DANGERS OF INVASION FROM WITHOUT, AND CONVULSIONS WITHIN.

Let's continue the example, from the previous cause for revolution, in addressing this item from the Declaration of Independence.

The People in Maui, having been completely disempowered from choice over their environment, by a biased and incompetent federal judge, now have no lawful means of governing themselves or their homeland when it comes to weeds, dangerous plants or noxious plants. In the view of the corrupt and incompetent judge who dissolved Maui's local laws, Congress had completely taken over regulation of weeds and noxious plants, in order to protect all of the people of the United States, therefore, no local governments should be allowed to protect their citizens.

Theoretically, the doctrine of pre-emption applies only if the federal law is as least restrictive on local government as possible, and, only if the federal law provides an alternative to local government. In essence, when the federal government proclaims that it is "pre-empting" local law on issues, it is saying to the People: "We've got your back." This, however, has become a mere ruse under current federal law and policy.

Theoretically, the federal government is allowed to dissolve the powers of Maui County, because it has set up the Food & Drug Administration to regulate all aspects of weeds in the United States. In theory, this sounds good. However, in reality, it is a mere sham.

For example, the current head of the FDA is Michael Taylor. He is the former head lobbyist for Monsanto, and a former Monsanto Vice President. No laws that regulate Monsanto will be passed without the permission of the FDA head. No regulations that may have ANY effect on Monsanto's profits will be passed, OR EN-

FORCED, because the FDA is a "captive agency." A captive agency is a government regulatory body that is controlled by the very industry that it purports to regulate.

In other words, through a corrupt and incompetent judiciary, and a corrupt and incompetent Food & Drug Administration, the federal government has effectively dissolved the County of Maui's ability to protect its own citizens from weeds, noxious plants or dangerous plants.

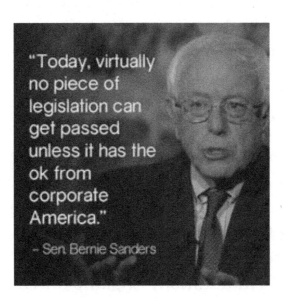

VII. HE HAS ENDEAVOURED TO PREVENT

THE POPULATION OF THESE STATES;
FOR THAT PURPOSE OBSTRUCTING
THE LAWS FOR NATURALIZATION OF
FOREIGNERS; REFUSING TO PASS
OTHERS TO ENCOURAGE THEIR MI-
GRATIONS HITHER, AND RAISING
THE CONDITIONS OF NEW APPRO-
PRIATIONS OF LANDS.

One does not have to look far, in our modern situation in America, to find the parallel to this reason for the American Revolution.

This aspect of tyranny was as prevalent in colonial America as it is today.

England's wealthy, and King George, wanted to force Americans to pay high prices for British goods and services. Americans had an abundance of land and natural resources, but, few willing to endure the hardships of Colonial life as labor. In addition, England's wealthy wanted to sell slaves to Americans.

Americans saw a ready opportunity for expansion, and, increasing the number of workers in the Colonies by admitting immigrants. However, to protect England's version of America's current day ruling class (the 1%), King George refused to allow immigration into America on reasonable terms.

Today, America still has an abundance of land (despite overcrowding in cities). One half of the world's population lives inside of a circle that is about the same geographic surface area of the U.S. That circle is in the Pacific basin centered around Beijing. Geographically, America could easily support ten times its current population. In terms of natural resources, America still has an abundance of them to the point that it could internally support, at least, three and half times of its current population.

America's current bottleneck to supporting a higher population is its infrastructure.

Since World War II, the great infrastructure built by American labor has slowly deteriorated so that the 1% can exploit its profits by using our infrastructure without having to pay to maintain, sustain or improve that infrastructure.

Looking at Congress in the past 40 years, we can see progressive amounts of enormously complicated laws that have one purpose and one purpose only. That purpose is to shift the burden of maintaining and building or infrastructure on to the middle class, and the poor, (through heavy taxation of middle income people and through austerity programs for the poor).

In the midst of this crushing tax strategy, and burden on the middle class, is a large pool of undocumented aliens in the U.S. By most estimates, there are 11 million undocumented aliens within our borders. This huge number of people has no path to legal immigration status because of the repressive failure of Congress, intentionally, to pass immigration reform.

Why?

The answer is very simple. The 1% rejoices in having a huge pool of undocumented immigrants in the U.S. Those undocumented aliens to survive, must work. They represent a huge class of exploitable labor. Not only are they themselves exploited (sometimes in literal conditions of slavery) but they represent a huge economic force depressing wages for the poor and middle class citizens of the U.S. This depression of wages for U.S. citizens is a key element in the 1% retaining economic power of the United States. The lower the wages, the more money the ruling class in the U.S. can keep for itself.

The lower the wages of American workers, the closer American workers are to desperate economic circumstances. The more American workers are close to desperate economic circumstances, the more they are dependent upon loans from the 1%, government subsidies, and the large banking interests in this country.

Cleverly, the corporate controlled media in this country, through selective reporting, keeps pointing the finger of blame for this situation upon the "illegal aliens" who have "flooded this country." This pretense perpetuates the racial tension in this country, and, successfully divides the electorate along racial lines. "Divide and conquer" has served the 1% well over the past 40 years as they can easily divide American voters, by means of a corporate controlled mass media, along any number of lines, including race, nationality, gender and economic status. Once American voters are distracted by the division, the 1% and the ruling class are able to get any laws passed that they please, and, any government support that they please.

To prevent this, it becomes our responsibility, as Americans to no longer foolishly allow ourselves to be divided.

As President John F. Kennedy pointed out, in his brilliant work "A Nation of Immigrants," this country is founded and anchored in the labors of Peoples who have come from all over the world.

We are a **nation of immigrants**. For generations, families braved treacherous paths, often fleeing unspeakable poverty and violence, in search of **better futures**, for **better lives** for their children.

Bernie   BERNIESANDERS.COM

Yet, time and time again, conservative elements in our country, trying to maintain a stranglehold on personal wealth, our natural resources, our once great infrastructure, and our labor force, have been successful in employing the corporate controlled mass media to divide us along racial lines, economic lines and political ideologies.

In reality, America's frustration with joblessness, low wages for American workers, long
hours, high costs of living and consumer inflation do not belong on the shoulders of undocumented aliens. America's frustrations belong on
the shoulders of the 1%, and corporate multinationals, who are intentionally using trade
agreements to drive American jobs overseas to
the Pacific Basin, while at the same time promoting undocumented aliens who will work for
30-40% of the wages that Americans deserve for
the same jobs.

Senator Sanders is the only presidential candidate who fully understands the problems facing Americans as a result of a passive-aggressive
refusal, on the part of conservatives and the 1%,
to provide a meaningful path to citizenship for
those workers who come to this country.

Senator Sanders proposes a limited amnesty
for those who are in the U.S. illegally. That amnesty would carry conditions for remaining in
the U.S. that are sensible. Those conditions
would allow immigrants to participate in our
economy, at real wages, and require the 1% to
pay all workers the same level of wages for the
same work. This would end the effect of 11 mil-

lion undocumented aliens who, for survival, must work for substandard wages. These same undocumented aliens, as a condition of their path to citizenship, would be required, finally, to pay into our healthcare system. This would further reduce the burden on the poor, the taxpayers and the middle class that results from irrationally excluding undocumented immigrants from the legitimate economy.

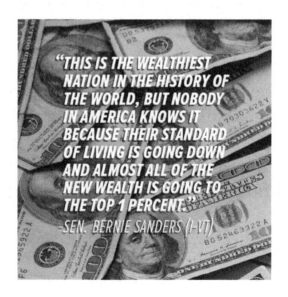

"THIS IS THE WEALTHIEST NATION IN THE HISTORY OF THE WORLD, BUT NOBODY IN AMERICA KNOWS IT BECAUSE THEIR STANDARD OF LIVING IS GOING DOWN AND ALMOST ALL OF THE NEW WEALTH IS GOING TO THE TOP 1 PERCENT."
-SEN. BERNIE SANDERS (I-VT)

With citizenship, or, even with 11 million undocumented workers on a path towards citizenship, these workers can emerge from the underground economy, earn more wages, pay taxes that they are not now paying, pay for their medical care and insurance, relieve our overburdened immigration courts, and relieve us of the huge expense of anti-immigration agencies, and join Americans. American workers will then no longer have their wages suppressed, by an underground labor force, and wages will rise in the U.S. for everyone. Without a path to citizenship for this huge underground economy of undocumented aliens, the 1% wins again, and, most workers in the U.S. earn about half the wages to which they are entitled.

VIII. HE HAS OBSTRUCTED THE ADMIN-ISTRATION OF JUSTICE, BY REFUSING HIS ASSENT TO LAWS FOR ESTABLISHING JUDICIARY POWERS.

This reason for our founders revolting against King George revolves around the King refusing to allow colonials to have a court system. Colonials felt that civilization requires a system of determining right and wrong, apprehending criminals, and providing a means of settling private disputes. King George refused to allow courts in Colonial America (in part because he feared that American courts might impose justice on British citizens and British companies).

In the U.S., today, we have a similar problem. Although we have a court system, that court system is "stacked" with political appointees who are literally dedicated to serving the ruling class and the 1%.

A revolt is justified against the entire justice system in America, and the judiciary, not because they don't exist, but, because our judiciary has become so corrupt, and incompetent, that America's court system is worse than what exists in many third world countries.

Dark money is at the root of judicial corruption and incompetence in the U.S. Arguably, our system of judges is so corrupt and incompetent that they are responsible for more harm to American citizens than would occur if there was no judiciary.

Most Americans find it difficult to believe this, until they are entangled in the judicial system (something that is almost inevitable in our modern times). The culprit in this deterioration of our judges and judicial system lies in several sources.

The first reason for our corrupt judiciary is the incredibly poor legal education that lawyers and judges receive in the U.S.

In the 1970's, American universities discovered that law schools generated huge profits for universities. All that was required were classrooms, a break room, a library and some teachers with law degrees. As a result, most universities in the U.S. opened a law school. Our education system began turning out ten times the amount of lawyers that are needed in our society. The result was that a lawyer's employability had nothing to do with his or her competence or integrity. A lawyer's employability depended completely on his or her ability to generate profits, for big law firms, that served the interests of the 1%. Only about 1 out of 40 lawyers who graduated under this system ever received well-paying jobs. Those 1 out of 40 became predators on the legal system in favor of reinforcing and sustaining the ruling class.

Our current pool of judges has been drawn from these single-minded predators. Their qualifications are simply that they have the same single-minded political ideologies of those in power who appointed them.

The end result of this corruption is that we no longer have a system based upon the "rule of law."

Although we have millions of laws, each of those laws is open to interpretation. You can go in front of a Republican judge, for instance, and obtain the exact **opposite** ruling that you would receive if you had gone before a Democratic judge. Under our current system of "law," our judges are free to disregard any law, or, any rule they please. Some courts are so corrupt and incompetent as to have actually come out and hold that rules or laws are nothing more than "suggestions" or "guidelines" for judges.

In addition to being able to disregard any law a judge may please, judges are free to disregard any facts or evidence they please. If a judge does not want evidence to influence the outcome of a case, the judge has numerous rules upon which the judge can exclude the evidence. Excluding evidence that contradicts the judge's biases and political ideologies guarantees the outcome of the case in favor of the judge's pre-ordained biases and prejudices. This means that judicial decisions can be based upon nothing more than a story the judge has made up about what really happened in a civil or criminal case.

Although appellate courts are supposed to prevent this, most of the time they do nothing. Appellate judges usually just read over the trial judge's opinion, and, if it sounds reasonable to them, they affirm the trial judge's ruling. Occasionally a case will hit a hot button with appellate judges and they will overturn the case. However, the majority of the time, they do nothing to investigate what the actual evidence proved, or, whether the trial judge applied it to all of the laws that should be applied.

This is true not only in lawsuits, but, also in criminal cases.

The judges of this country have, literally, abolished all checks and balances on their own power. They have given themselves "absolute power."

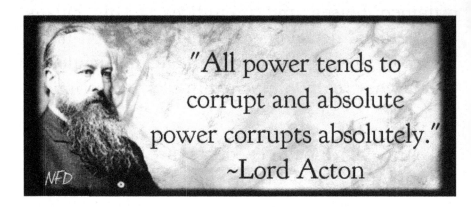

"All power tends to corrupt and absolute power corrupts absolutely." ~Lord Acton

The result is an incarceration rate that is the highest in the known history of humanity, as well as a system of courts that serves only the wealthy and powerful.

Criminal trials have become nothing more than formalities with convictions being almost assured in most cases. [9]

With convictions almost assured, by corrupt and incompetent judges, Senator Sanders notes

---

[9] The U.S. Department of "Justice" boasts that it is able to coerce 95% of accused persons to accept guilty pleas, irrespective whether the person is, or is not, guilty under due process standards. Bar-Gill, Oren & Gazel, Oren, Plea Bargains Only for the Guilty, Discussion Paper 481, Harvard Center for Law, Economics and Business, (June 2006). This paper can be downloaded without charge from: The Harvard John M. Olin Discussion Paper Series: http://www.law.harvard.edu/programs/olin_center/

that we must bring back a system of federal paroles so that there is a check and balance on the judges who are dedicated to serving high conviction rates rather than due process.

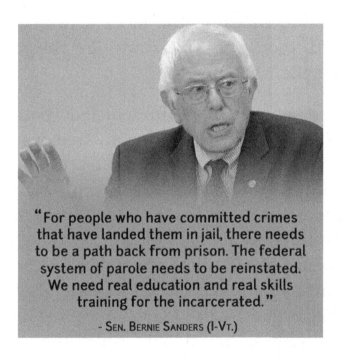

"For people who have committed crimes that have landed them in jail, there needs to be a path back from prison. The federal system of parole needs to be reinstated. We need real education and real skills training for the incarcerated."

- SEN. BERNIE SANDERS (I-VT.)

IX. HE HAS MADE JUDGES DEPENDENT ON HIS WILL ALONE, FOR THE TENURE OF THEIR OFFICES, AND THE AMOUNT AND PAYMENT OF THEIR

SALARIES.

In Colonial America, all of the judges were essentially employees of the King. If a judge did not decide cases on the basis of what the King wanted, then, the King could fire the judges, or reduce their salaries.

In response, the Founders incorporated into our Constitution[10] a provision that would keep judges completely unaccountable to anyone, especially the President. This was originally intended to protect the people from a President who wanted to act as a king or tyrant. However, in modern times, this "protection" in the Constitution has been turned on its ear. Judges now are appointed by the "King" [the President], and the Congress, based only upon their absolute loyalties to a system that is corruptly under the complete control of the 1%. As a result, judges are completely unaccountable to the People. The court system in the U.S. is effectively under the complete control of the 1% because the 1% have complete control over the politicians who

---

[10] Article III, Section 1

appoint judges.

The judges then, having absolute power, and accountable to no one, proceed to rule on cases affecting millions of individuals in the U.S., but only ruling on those cases in a way that suits their own prejudices and biases, and, the agendas of the ruling class. We need a revolt to change this so that judges, once again, grant ordinary citizens the rights to due process of law.

X. HE HAS ERECTED A MULTITUDE OF NEW OFFICES, AND SENT HITHER SWARMS OF OFFICERS TO HARASS OUR PEOPLE, AND EAT OUT THEIR SUBSTANCE.

In Colonial America, the King set up customs agencies and admiralty agencies. The ostensible purpose of these agencies was to regulate (serve and protect") the colonies from unscrupulous overseas trade practices.

What happened, however, is that these agencies became "captive agencies" . . . they came under the complete control of the business people in England that they were supposed to regulate.

What was supposed to be an honest system of regulation was turned against Colonials in favor of British wealthy interests.

We don't have to look far in modern times to find the same phenomenon in the U.S.

The Internal Revenue "Service" is a good example. The Internal Revenue Service is supposed to fairly administer the tax code so that everyone pays their fair share of taxes.

In reality, however, the IRS really only enforces the tax code against the middle class and workers. Wealthy individuals and large corporations have the money to hire lawyers to fight the IRS in court, so the IRS focuses on terrorizing middle class taxpayers to force them to pay the bulk of taxes from their earnings.

At the same time, proponents of "trickle down economics" keep insisting that by lowering taxes on wealthy individuals and companies will lead to the formation of more jobs for workers and enhance America's prosperity for everyone.

Forty years of economic decline, for workers, the poor, and the middle class in America, and a national deb of 19 Trillion dollars, is the result of this epic failure of economic and tax strategy in the U.S.

When the ruling class has extra money from low tax rates, the ruling class does not create jobs in the U.S. The ruling class takes that money and buys itself influence in other countries where wages are a tiny fraction of what they are in the U.S. They then "downsize" in the U.S. by eliminating millions of American jobs. They create factories and businesses in other countries where their profits cannot be taxed by the U.S. People.

This leaves the American middle class and the working poor, in America, to pay for the entire infrastructure that the ruling class uses in the U.S. to produce their wealth.

However, the IRS rarely pursues tax cases against wealthy individuals or multi-national corporations. Most of its enforcement efforts are directed solely against the middle class who provides the bulk of revenues for the U.S.

The IRS, in America, joins over 22 million federal, state, and local government employees who enforce laws, selectively, mostly against the poor and middle class, while rarely enforcing laws against the 1% or the ruling class.

XI. HE HAS KEPT AMONG US, IN TIMES OF PEACE, STANDING ARMIES WITHOUT THE CONSENT OF OUR LEGISLATURES.

In Colonial times, there was no such thing as a civilian police force. The concept of a civilian police force eventually developed to track down, capture and return escaped slaves to their owners.[11] King George, however, decided that he

---

[11] Potter, Gary, THE HISTORY OF POLICING IN THE UNITED STATES, 2015. ("In the Southern states the development of American policing followed a different path. The genesis of the modern police organization in the South is the "Slave Patrol" (Platt 1982). The first formal slave patrol was created in the Carolina colonies in 1704 (Reichel 1992). Slave patrols had three primary functions: (1)

needed to use violence to enforce his laws, and, allowed a standing army, which he had used against the French, to remain in the colonies for "law and order."

The military enforcement of the King's civil laws turned out to be brutal. It was a military style of "justice" (not unlike the rubber stamp criminal courts we have in the U.S. today) with floggings,[12] and hangings perpetrated on colonials at the whim of the military commander.

It is for this reason that the U. S. Constitution (combined with a principal of law known as "*posse comitatus* (power to local governments),"[13] strictly limits (even prohibits) the use of the U.S.

---

to chase down, apprehend, and return to their owners, runaway slaves; (2) to provide a form of organized terror to deter slave revolts; and, (3) to maintain a form of discipline for slave-workers who were subject to summary justice, outside of the law, if they violated any plantation rules. Following the Civil War, these vigilante-style organizations evolved in modern Southern police departments primarily as a means of controlling freed slaves who were now laborers working in an agricultural caste system, and enforcing "Jim Crow" segregation laws, designed to deny freed slaves equal rights and access to the political system."

[12] Although we no longer have "floggings" we allow our prisons to impose various forms of torture on prisoners, such as unlimited solitary confinement, and, unlimited authorization of prison guards to dehumanize prisoners.

[13] 18 U.S.C. § 1385 (2015).

Military against the citizens of the United States.

Surely there are no standing armies in the U.S. to be used against its citizens by those in power . . .. or are there?

The militarization of American police has been documented in the mainstream media for over fifty years. Police use military weapons, often provided by the Department of Defense. Police wear uniforms and assign themselves military rank. Even the smallest town has a police chief, or Sheriff, who arraigns themselves in the glory of a four star general.

Although we do not use the branches of the armed forces to police citizens, fascist elements in our culture have succeeded in finding substitutes, such as the police and the National Guard, that are for all practical purposes paramilitary organizations.

The Supreme Court, in what could be described as treachery against the American People, have given the police all of the arbitrary and capricious authority of a military dictator. They have done this by rulings that created certain standards of law which abandon due process for the People of the United States.

The Supreme Court, for example, has invented the "reasonable fear" standard for police violence against citizens. In short, if any law enforcement officer "feels" that his life is in danger, for any reason, he may use deadly force to kill a citizen. There is no due process of law required. All that is required, to use deadly force, is merely the completely whimsical feeling of fear on the part of law enforcement.

With this standard, it is almost completely impossible to obtain a conviction of an officer of the law when that officer murders a civilian. All that is necessary for a police officer to justify his murder of a civilian is for him to claim he was "afraid" and show some things in the situation which might justify is "fear."

Almost anyone can justify their "fears." However, the police now are a privileged class that is permitted to murder for no other reason than that they are "afraid."

In his platform, Senator Sanders wisely proposed that there be strict, and objective rules for when a police officer can, or cannot, use deadly force.

XII. HE HAS AFFECTED TO RENDER THE MILITARY INDEPENDENT OF AND SUPERIOR TO THE CIVIL POWER.

This portion of the Declaration of Independence refers to the appointment of a military governor in the colonies who was completely unaccountable to the people in colonial America.

The obvious parallel, today, is the fact that our militarized police force is almost completely above the law.

Most Americans, swept up in the mass media's frenzy of promoting "law and order," had no idea that having a militarized police force would eventually be turned against all of the people by anyone who could merely think of an accusation. Literally tens of thousands of television shows, and movies, have glorified the "Dirty Harry" mentality that became so popular in the 1970's. Many Americans, because of racism, assumed that the militarized police in the U.S. would be used against minorities, or poor people, and that white, middle class America would be left alone.

Americans, who thought the police would only go after criminals, created a police state in which ordinary citizens, going about their daily lives, commit multiple crimes everyday without ever intending to commit crimes.

The corrupt and incompetent Supreme Court has encouraged lawmakers to make laws that criminalize behavior by ordinary citizens which amount to nothing more than mistakes.

Figure 1 – "Four star generals" are in charge of the people of even the smallest towns in America.

In the "law and order" hysteria that followed the "Dirty Harry" phenomenon, our "leaders" passed legislation in such abundance that, virtually, almost everything is now a crime. Middle class America is now as much under attack as minorities have been for the past 45 years, by a militarized body of police that is out of control, and, effectively accountable to no one.

Small town governments, to the federal government, have now turned to criminal law enforcement, and millions of armed police soldiers, to collect additional revenues for themselves. Quota ticketing schemes have become commonplace all over America . . . and "asset forfeiture" (which is nothing more than pure theft) has become a way for "law enforcement" to aggrandize itself, financially, through the shakedown of ordinary Americans (including minorities).

This police state power is completely under the control of the 1% and the ruling class.

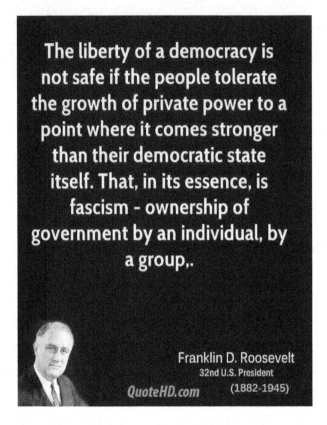

The liberty of a democracy is not safe if the people tolerate the growth of private power to a point where it comes stronger than their democratic state itself. That, in its essence, is fascism - ownership of government by an individual, by a group,.

Franklin D. Roosevelt
32nd U.S. President
(1882-1945)

QuoteHD.com

The police are no longer an instrument that "protects and serves" the people . . . The police are now only an instrument of the ruling class to keep the People of the United States "in line."

Figure 2 - The police chief of Santa Monica, California arraigns herself as a four-star general.

Is it an exaggeration to say this this occupying military force is above the law? Not really. Our Supreme Court has established standards for police that are so low, that our court system in the United States, which is supposed to protect our individual liberties, has become nothing more than a rubber stamp for the militarized police.

This trend began with Chief Justice William Rehnquist who made the remark, off the record, "We will establish law and order no matter what expense to individual liberties." His learned predecessors called this "fascism." However, the blind hysteria, fueled by the mass media, completed the ability of the plutocracy to make fascism the reality of everyday life in America (enforced by the violence of a militarized police force).

We must demilitarize our police forces so they don't look and act like invading armies.

Bernie

XIII. HE HAS COMBINED WITH OTHERS TO SUBJECT US TO A JURISDICTION FOREIGN TO OUR CONSTITUTION, AND UNACKNOWLEDGED BY OUR LAWS; GIVING HIS ASSENT TO THEIR ACTS OF PRETENDED LEGISLATION:

This referenced the fact that King George, and his wealthy sponsors, enlisted the help of the British Parliament to pass laws governing the colonists. These laws were supposed to be in conformance with the British Constitution. However, the laws were nothing more than laws pretending to be fair. In fact they were laws that were designed to exploit the colonials, impose enormous economic burdens on them, and, deprive them of any effective means of organizing against the King's interests (and the interests of those who controlled the King).

We don't have to look far in America, today, to see parallels in pretended laws that impose burdens on Americans for the benefit of the wealthy who corrupt Congress, the White House, and the Supreme Court.

Laws passed for "national security" are perhaps the best example of this type of pretended legislation.

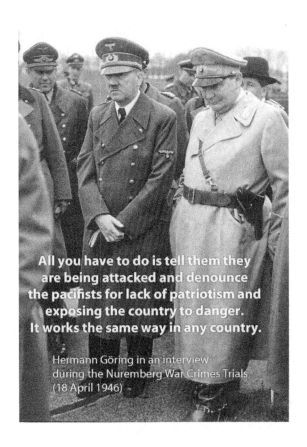

All you have to do is tell them they are being attacked and denounce the pacifists for lack of patriotism and exposing the country to danger. It works the same way in any country.

Hermann Göring in an interview during the Nuremberg War Crimes Trials (18 April 1946)

The corporate controlled mass media, and the government, because it is in their interests, create environments of paranoia, and hysteria, among Americans.

To address the paranoia they created, they have passed draconian laws that remove, virtually, every freedom that Americans once enjoyed. These same laws create a police state, in the name of "law and order," in which any person, for almost any reason, can be accused of a crime and put in prison under harsh terms.

This has been the successful ruse and mechanism for every tyranny in history. This ruse is no more prevalent in the world, anywhere today, than it is in the U.S.

XIV. FOR QUARTERING LARGE BODIES OF ARMED TROOPS AMONG US:

In reaction to the Boston Tea Party, King George responded by, among other things, requiring American citizens to pay for the housing of the troops that he intended to use to maintain "law and order" in the colonies.

Are "large bodies of armed troops among us?" Let's take a look at all of the government agencies that have "guns and badges" to "establish law and order" (keep the people of the United States in line):

> *The most recent report from the Bureau of Justice Statistics quadrennial "Census of State and Local Law Enforcement Agencies, 2008" shows that there were over 1.1 million persons employed on a full-time basis by state and local law enforcement in this country in 2008. Of that number, about 765,000 were sworn personnel—which is defined as those with general arrest powers.*
>
> *The report contains data from 17,985 state and local law enforcement agencies with at least one full-time officer or the equivalent in part-time officers, including:*
>
> *12,501 local police departments*
> *3,063 sheriffs' offices*
> *50 primary state law enforcement agencies*
> *1,733 special jurisdiction agencies*
> *683 other agencies, primarily county constable offices in Texas.[14]*

---

[14] Alaska Justice Forum, University of Alaska, U.S. STATE AND LOCAL LAW ENFORCEMENT AGENCIES CENSUS 2008: A BJS REPORT http://justice.uaa.alaska.edu/forum/28/2-3summerfall2011/f_lawenf_census.html

These totals do not include federal law enforcement agencies. If we reference the most recent federal census on law enforcement in the U.S. (taken in 2008), the U.S. Department of Justice, Bureau of Justice Statistics (BJS) reports the following:

Highlights:

- *State and local law enforcement agencies employed about 1,133,000 persons on a full-time basis in 2008, including 765,000 sworn personnel.*
- *About half (49%) of all agencies employed fewer than 10 full-time officers. Nearly two-thirds (64%) of sworn personnel worked for agencies that employed 100 or more officers.*
- *From 2004 to 2008, state and local law enforcement agencies added about 9,500 more full-time sworn personnel than during the previous 4-year period*

This is roughly one armed law enforcement person for every 330 man, woman and child in the United States.

If we consult the surveys for federal law enforcement officers, we can add another 120,000 gun carrying, badge wielding, persons who occupy the U.S. on behalf of the ruling class. The federal Bureau of Justice Statistics has the following to say:

> *In September 2008, federal agencies employed approximately 120,000 full-time law enforcement officers who were authorized to make arrests and carry firearms in the United States.*[15]

If this list of "law enforcement agencies" does not qualify as an "occupying army" against the people of the United States, by the ruling class, it would be impossible to conceive of something that **does** qualify as an "occupying army."

If this army of "law enforcement" officers were present, in the U.S., to genuinely "protect and serve," then there might be some justification for such massive use of force and violence against the people of the United States.

The past forty years, however, has shown that the "law enforcement community" in the U.S. is entirely controlled by the wealthy ruling class, and, directed against the People by relentless propaganda in the corporate controlled me-

---

[15] Reaves, Ph.D., Brian A., "*Federal Law Enforcement Officers 2008*," Bureau of Justice Statistics, U.S. Department of Justice, June 2012. http://www.bjs.gov/content/pub/pdf/fleo08.pdf

dia.

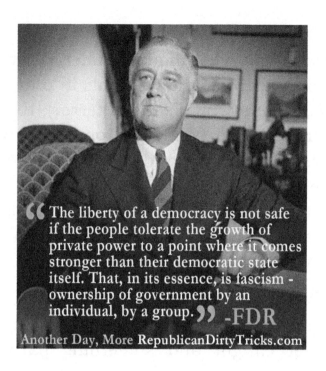

The liberty of a democracy is not safe if the people tolerate the growth of private power to a point where it comes stronger than their democratic state itself. That, in its essence, is fascism - ownership of government by an individual, by a group. -FDR

Another Day, More RepublicanDirtyTricks.com

XV. FOR PROTECTING THEM, BY A MOCK TRIAL, FROM PUNISHMENT FOR ANY MURDERS WHICH THEY SHOULD COMMIT ON THE INHABITANTS OF THESE STATES:

Viewing our tens of thousands of police agencies in the U.S., as an occupying army, provides a direct parallel with this provision of the Declaration of Independence.

In Colonial America, the occupying troops that the ruling class had in America, were instructed to terrorize the colonials in order to enforce, *in terroram* (by means of terror), the will of the ruling class in London. Consequently, they went out brutalizing and murdering colonials "by the bushel." When the colonials fought back, or defended themselves, the ruling class in England used it as an excuse to step up the brutality and murder in order to establish "law and order."

Occasionally, the British law enforcement would get caught and something particularly atrocious in terms of murder and brutality against colonials. To quell riots and prevent armed insurrection, the King and his plutocrats might begrudgingly charge the soldiers (police) with a crime.

The King, however, and his British business supporters (the ruling class in Colonial America) owned all of the judges. All of the judges were appointed by the ruling class in England, and, owed money to the King and his supporters. The result was that any trial of the police, in colonial America, was merely a mock trial to try to persuade the colonials that the British police (soldiers) had not really committed any atrocities.

This is exactly the situation that we have today in the U.S. The police in the U.S. are owned and controlled by the wealthy and the U.S. plutocracy. They serve wealthy insurance companies and banks. The police in the U.S. are glorified in the corporate controlled media. The judges in the U.S. consider police to be their loyal and worthy servants who enhance the judge's power, and the prosecutors are consider dashing darlings who are without blemish. Convictions of police who murder and brutalize Americans have, therefore, become almost impossible. The prosecutors and the judges will throw cases in favor of the police at every opportunity to assure that they are acquitted of even the most obvious atrocities. That is why police usually waive a jury trial and elect to be tried before a judge . . . (Acquittal of a police officer is almost assured before a judge who derives his power from the brutal and militarized police force).

Even if a law enforcement person is convicted, judges will typically hand down sweetheart sentences.

Is it an exaggeration to say that trials against

accused police in the U.S. are "mock trials?"

To be certain, there are cases in which police are held accountable for crimes against civilians. However, those cases are so few that they should almost be disregarded as examples of police accountability.

Usually, police are never even charged when they murder and brutalize Americans.

One of the deceitful and fraudulent methods that prosecutors and judges use, to exonerate murderous or criminal police officers, is to take the accusation before a grand jury.

Many people misunderstand what a "grand jury" is. People mistakenly think that an entire fair trial occurs during a grand jury proceeding. Nothing could be further from the truth.

There is no judge in grand jury proceedings. There are no defense attorneys. There is no open inspection of the fairness of the proceeding as they are secret. The secrecy was originally intended to protect the jurors. However, now, that same secrecy protects corrupt prosecutors who want, at all costs, to make sure that police are never charged for their crimes.

Only the prosecutor is present in a grand jury proceeding. He can decide, all by himself, to keep out any information and evidence from a jury (especially evidence of the guilt of the police) that he pleases. He can use facial expressions, tone of voice and thousands of other "sleights of hand" to make it clear to the jury that he doesn't want them to find that the police have committed any crime. There is nothing present in a grand jury proceeding to keep the prosecutor from committing this fraud.

Once the grand jury has decided, based upon the prosecutors' clever fraud, that the police did not commit a crime, the prosecutor then announces to the media, and the public, that the grand jury refused to indict the officer because the officer is innocent. This is an outrageous sham and it is so common that few police, if ever, have to face trials for their crimes. The grand jury, in effect, operates as a mock trial to clear the police so that they never face charges or the evidence against them.

What does a "mock trial" look like in modern day America?

In November of 2012, a Black couple was riding in their car in Cleveland. The car backfired and police began chasing them. In all, 62 police cars joined in pursuing them based on the assumption that the backfire was a gunshot. The couple had committed no crimes other than minor traffic offenses during the chase. The couple was completely unarmed.

When the couple (probably terrified of the police) finally stopped the car, the police peremptorily fired 137 rounds into the vehicle. One of the officers fired 47 of the shots at the vehicle. The murdering officer emptied his high capacity magazines 3 times, into the occupants, while he was standing on the hood of the vehicle. He could see through the windshield that the couple inside was unarmed. He jumped on the car and fired with his legs spread, through the windshield, at the couple, with the intent to kill.

He was charged with manslaughter. He waived a jury trial and proceeded to a trial before a white male judge. The officer was a white male.

After the trial the judge found that the officer was "innocent" because he had a reasonable fear for his life. The judge "reasoned" that all of the shooting being done by the other policemen and the large number of police vehicles surrounding the black couple's car gave the police officer on the hood of the car a "reason" to be "afraid."

That is what a mock trial looks like.

Effectively, anything can serve as a reasonable basis for fear of the officer's safety, consequently, the Supreme Court, and judges, have placed the police above the law, and, citizens have no protection from police brutality or police murder of unarmed civilians.

Hemingway reminds us, in one of his treatises, that throughout history, no government that has used deadly force against its own people has ever survived.

XVI. FOR CUTTING OFF OUR TRADE WITH ALL PARTS OF THE WORLD:

In the Colonies, the King sought to control the entire economy in his favor, and in favor of his cronies. This included a system of taxation that favored the large British commercial empire that would soon, with the British military, focus on crushing the Continental economy. The Continental economy, in Europe, emerged when France followed the U.S. in revolution. The British wealthy and its ruling class were, literally, terrified that the American Revolution and the incipient French revolution would spread to England.

The King's efforts, against Americans, included closing the Boston harbor after the Boston tea party, and, massive amounts of regulation and laws aimed at crippling the Colonial economy to the extent that it, in any way, challenged the British ruling class.

Yet, as unfamiliar as this may seem to us today, that is exactly what the ruling class has done to middle class and poor Americans.

Beginning in the early 1980's, America's ruling class began a war on the American worker. This started with Reagan making a concerted effort to destroy unions, promote trade with low wage countries that employed slave labor, and setting up Americans to compete for jobs against the lowest paid workers in the world.

The excuse for this strategy was to flood America with a supply of cheap foreign goods, through retailers such as Walmart. It was called "supply side economics." The result has been that Americans can no longer find livable wage jobs, and, are forced to trade with multinationals to buy goods. The multinationals and the ruling class now insure that most profits in the U.S. are funneled to the ruling class and no one else.

Walmart, the largest retailer in the U.S., for example, ships billions of tons of goods from China and Southeast Asia into the U.S. When Walmart sets up a store in a neighborhood, it instantly drives hundreds of local businesses out of business. Walmart has been responsible for eliminating over 60,000 manufacturers in the U.S. Those manufacturers were the backbone of American employment, and, were once owned by the great middle class of America.

Walmart hires mostly part-time employees so that they can get around fair labor laws. Walmart pays such low wages that many of its employees must have support from public programs, at the taxpayers expense, to survive. Every underpaid employee of Walmart not only suppresses wages for every worker in the U.S., it also is a tax on those in the middle class, and the poor, who pay taxes on their own wages to support Walmart employees on welfare.

Americans must buy at Walmart because the ruling class has subsidized Walmart, at our expense, and because Walmart destroys American jobs. Americans can't trade anywhere else except at Walmart and the stores that imitate Walmart. Walmart has eliminated all small businesses that might compete with it by flooding the American market with cheap, and substandard, Chinese goods. Because Americans are now so poorly paid as workers, they have no choice but to buy at the cheapest retailers like Walmart.

In this way, and thousands of other ways, Americans have been cutoff from honest competitive trade in the U.S. In addition, American workers are now being forced to compete with slave-wage workers, in other countries, in order to have jobs in the U.S.

This, combined with competition from 11 million undocumented alien workers already in the U.S., the American worker now has a standard of living that is less than half the quality it was during the 1960's. American workers have no choice. American workers have been set up so that they cannot trade for a reasonable value of their work and services.

XVII. FOR IMPOSING TAXES ON US WITH-OUT OUR CONSENT:

This reference in the Declaration is about the British Parliament imposing the "Stamp Tax Act" on the colonists in 1765. The only purpose of the tax was to raise money for the ruling class in Britain. The tax was imposed without any of the consent of the Colonial governing bodies, or any of the Colonial citizens.

This led to the Founders of our nation creating the concept of not only no taxation without representation, but, that there should be NO government action without the consent of the governed.

Surely, with 450 representatives in the House of Representatives, and 100 Senators in the Senate, Americans have representation - don't they?

Surely, by numerous elections, Americans have given their consent to the Reagan era destruction of American workers, the rise of the police state during the Clinton era, the massive unfunded wars in the Middle East during the GW Bush era, and the bailout of banks and Wall Street in the U.S. during Obama's rule. Or did American's give their consent?

There is an ancient and well-established rule of law that fraud vitiates consent.

Arguably, the corporate controlled media in the U.S. has been committing a fraud on the public for decades.

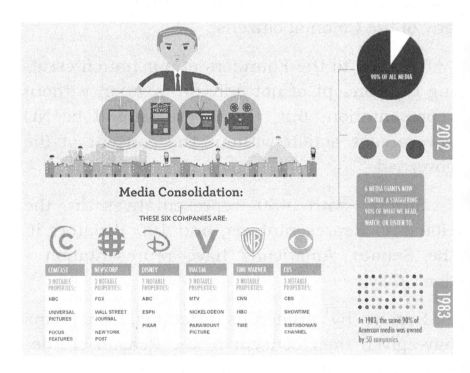

Figure 3 - Info graphic showing that only 6 corporations in the U.S. now control everything that we read, see and hear.

In colonial times, information was a product of face-to-face association with other People in the community. Alternatively, people gained information from small local newspapers. There were no gatekeepers to information. That is one of the reasons why our First Amendment was designed to provide freedom of association **and** freedom of speech. It enabled the electorate and the citizens to freely exchange information without censorship, or the control of the privileged and elite ruling class.

However, with the 20th Century advent of mass media, we no longer obtain information from each other. We obtain information from centralized sources, all dominated and controlled by profit seeking multinational corporations, that have nothing in common with the day-to-day struggles of the People of America.

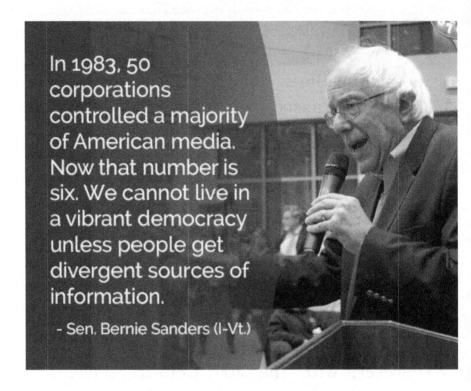

In 1983, 50 corporations controlled a majority of American media. Now that number is six. We cannot live in a vibrant democracy unless people get divergent sources of information.

- Sen. Bernie Sanders (I-Vt.)

Noam Chomsky, an MIT linguist and respected intellectual, describes this fraud by a controlled media as "manufactured consent."

With six large multinational corporations in complete control of mass media in the U.S., it is appropriate to question whether voters in the U.S. may be under the fraudulent influence of those corporations. Those corporations, as gate-keepers of information, exist solely to serve their own agendas (and the agendas of the ruling class that controls them).

We know from the spending on elections that now occurs, mostly by paying hundreds of millions of dollars to these six corporations, that this consolidated media machine has, arguably, controlled the election of representatives for the past 30 years. Have Americans really, freely elected their representatives? Or, have they been duped for decades by a corporate controlled mass media that manipulated voters to elect representatives that serve only the ruling class?

VIII. FOR DEPRIVING US IN MANY CASES, OF THE BENEFITS OF TRIAL BY JURY:

This part of the Declaration involves the ruling class in Britain inventing ways of punishing Colonists while denying them the right to a trial by jury. Under British law, anyone, including a Colonial, was entitled to be judged by a jury of his peers as opposed to being judged by government employees of the ruling class. Consequently, the British ruling class invented all kinds of new ways to punish Colonials with what are commonly known today as "administrative agencies."

The parallels to this, in our modern "justice system" are extraordinarily similar to what was occurring in Colonial America.

One good example is "child support enforcement" proceedings. The parent ordered to pay child support has no right to a trial by jury, and, in many cases, does not even have the right to introduce DNA evidence on the issue of paternity. Yet a judge can order a Father to prison, indefinitely, for not paying child support even if the Father is not the biological father of the child.

Young boys who are raped by older women, if the woman becomes pregnant, even though the boy is a victim of rape, are routinely ordered to pay child support. The rape victim has no right to a trial by jury, and, again, can be imprisoned indefinitely by a judge without any recourse to a trial by jury.

President Jefferson, in his writings, stated, "The right to a trial by jury is the anchor of democracy." However, instead, our judiciary has instituted a system of corrupt kangaroo courts that circumvent democracy.

The result is that many people (mostly men)

are now being imprisoned for "contempt" of agency orders. These men are not given any opportunity for a trial by jury as required in the Constitution.

AMERICA'S PRISON POPULATION

1972 — 300,000

2014 — 2,300,000

Source: Bureau of Justice Statistics   FRONTLINE

With our prison populations swelling, there are other ways in which Americans (mostly men and minority men) are deprived of their right to a trial by jury.

With the draconian sentencing punishments for even minor crimes, such as drug use or possession, many men are, literally, forced to plead guilty in cases in which juries may not convict.

This is done by threatening the accused with massive sentences if he does not plead "guilty." These plea offers are made to defendants when the prosecutor is not sure she can get a conviction at trial. Once the defendant pleads "guilty" to avoid being sentenced to decades in prison over minor offenses, he has waived all of his rights.

Our corrupt courts have then created a fiction to continue imprisoning Americans. The fiction is that since he has pleaded "guilty" he has no further protections under the law. The courts have held that his efforts to stay out of prison for parole or probation violations, or, for violating a plea agreement are merely "civil" matters to which the right to a trial by jury does not apply. The defendant then faces "rubber stamp" proceedings before a ruling class judge, instead of being fairly tried by a jury of his peers.

Through these charades of "justice" the ruling class provides an immense pipeline of prisoners to the private, for profit, prison industry in the U.S.

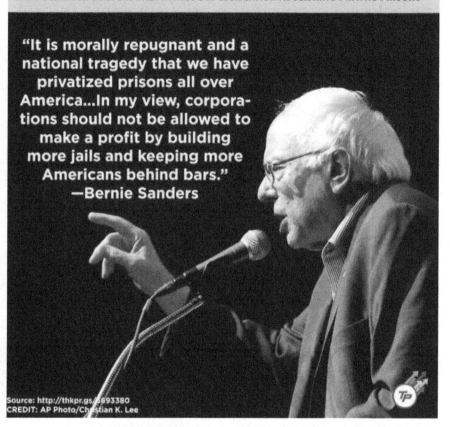

WHY SENTATOR SANDERS WILL INTRODUCE LEGISLATION ABOLISHING PRIVATE PRISONS

"It is morally repugnant and a national tragedy that we have privatized prisons all over America...In my view, corporations should not be allowed to make a profit by building more jails and keeping more Americans behind bars."
—Bernie Sanders

Source: http://thkpr.gs/3693380
CREDIT: AP Photo/Christian K. Lee

XIX. FOR TRANSPORTING US BEYOND SEAS TO BE TRIED FOR PRETENDED OF-FENCES.

The ruling class in Britain had decided that any colonial accused of a crime, against the ruling class (the King), would be arrested and brought to England to stand trial. Colonials were often arrested and transported to England to face trial before a prejudiced jury that was certain to rule in favor of the King and the ruling classes. In addition, it took about six months to make the trip to England, so, the accused Colonial had no real opportunity to call witnesses in his own defense.

Our own government does this today to the American People. One of the most obvious (though not very common) is the arrest of U.S. citizens in foreign countries, and, then holding them in secret prisons (such as Guantanamo) where they are beyond the reach of the assistance of any court, and any due process.

The truth is, however, the government also uses its resources, today, to make it impossible for ordinary citizens to reasonably defend themselves.

If the government decides to accuse someone of a crime, in the U.S., today, the government has almost unlimited state violence and economic resources to make sure that the person is found guilty (whether or not the person is actually guilty of a crime).

Let's look at some recent developments in state and federal prosecutions. After almost twenty years of FBI agents going on the witness stand in criminal cases, testifying that an accused was guilty based upon the "science" of hair identification, the FBI finally admitted that there is no such science, and, that over 4,000 men were convicted based upon the manufactured evidence. Jury pools in the U.S. have been brainwashed by thousands of TV shows and movies, to believe the FBI is professional and infallible. Four thousand juries fell for the fraudulent testimony in 4,000 cases.[16]

In Massachusetts, the head of a "crime lab" was caught falsifying lab results in over 40,000 cases. She was eventually prosecuted and sentenced to five years in prison, but, not before 40,000 people had served time in prison all, or most of whom, may have been innocent.[17]

Even if there is no outright fraud by the government, in criminal trials, overcharging by

---

[16] *FBI admits flaws in hair analysis over decades*, Washington Post, April 15, 2015.

[17] *CSI Is a Lie*, Atlantic Monthly, April 20, 2015.

prosecutors, based on flimsy evidence, and falsified police reports, often forces innocent people to plead guilty.

Innocent people plead guilty for all sorts of reasons. The biggest reason is that they can't afford to take the chance of going before a judge that will rubber stamp approval on the government's case, deny the constitutional arguments of defense counsel, and send signals to the jury that he wants them to convict the defendant. (Judges will often do this by refusing to respect the defense counsel so that he looks bad before the jury – there are thousands of ways for judges to do this, and they do it frequently). Judges look on prosecutors as heroes and part of their personal staff . . .. They look upon defense attorneys as being an annoyance to the government and little more than a formality for show. As one criminal trial judge once said: "Where is the public defender? We have to have a public defender or we can't send people to prison."

Just as King George removed often-innocent people to England to make sure they would not have a fair trial, our own government, today, has assembled a vast franchise of kangaroo courts that insure convictions and guilty pleas even if the accused is innocent.

The results are obvious. The U.S. now imprisons 25% of the world's prisoners . . .. 93% of them are men . . .. The vast majority of those men are minorities (especially African-Americans and Hispanics).

XX. FOR ABOLISHING THE FREE SYSTEM OF ENGLISH LAWS IN A NEIGHBOURING PROVINCE, ESTABLISHING THEREIN AN ARBITRARY GOVERNMENT, AND ENLARGING ITS BOUNDARIES SO AS TO RENDER IT AT ONCE AN EXAMPLE AND FIT INSTRUMENT FOR INTRODUCING THE SAME ABSOLUTE RULE INTO THESE COLONIES:

This particular reason for revolting against the King and his ruling class is a bit convoluted.

Knowing that the Colonials were going to revolt, in response to the ruling class' extreme measures to punish Colonials, Britain took some extraordinary steps.

The King, and his ruling class of wealthy individuals in England, made peace with the French in Quebec. He granted them extraordinary concessions so that he would have a staging area for an invasion of the colonies. Quebec would be the place the English Army could easily launch a full military invasion of the U.S. in the event the Colonials rebelled.

Fortunately, we have not yet reached this point in the U.S. in which the 1% and the ruling class have been preparing a full military invasion and martial law over Americans.

Fortunately, because of the enlightenment of our Founders, Americans have the avenue of a political revolution instead of military confrontation. At least we all hope this is the case.

XXI. FOR TAKING AWAY OUR CHARTERS, ABOLISHING OUR MOST VALUABLE LAWS, AND ALTERING FUNDAMENTALLY THE FORMS OF OUR GOVERNMENTS:

This reason for the Declaration of Independence centers on another legal retaliation against the Colonists by the King and the wealthy ruling class in England.

After the Boston Tea Party, to punish the Colonials, the ruling class in England and America conspired to deprive Colonials of such basic rights as a trial by jury.

Fortunately, the U.S. has not yet gotten to the point in which the ruling class is directly, and openly, repealing our Constitutional rights.

Fortunately, we have a chance through political revolution, with a leader like Senator Sanders, to reverse the trend of the ruling class undermining our Constitutional rights.

Senator Sanders, in his various platform proposals, has recognized the need for criminal justice reform, and, has introduced legislation to correct our current system of mass convictions and mass incarcerations.

XXII. FOR SUSPENDING OUR OWN LEGISLATURES, AND DECLARING THEMSELVES INVESTED WITH POWER TO LEGISLATE FOR US IN ALL CASES WHATSOEVER.

This reason for the American Revolution revolves around the King punishing Americans by dissolving their legislatures if colonies refused to house troops for the King and his ruling class.

We don't (yet) have a direct parallel in America, today. However, we have something similar.

It has become obvious to Americans that conservatives in Congress are simply politicians who have been bought by the wealthy and the ruling class. They have not outright dissolved Congress, however, to punish Americans for laws the benefit the People (such as a coherent plan of medical insurance) these corrupt politicians have shut down Congress, repeatedly over funding.

They routinely shut down Congress, and the

government, by holding us hostage over budget items.

These obstructionists are not representatives of the People of the United States. They are representatives only of special interests. Their obstructionist tactics are as effective and dissolving Congress to the extent that it could, otherwise, provide meaningful legislation for the People of America instead of its ruling class.

XIII. HE HAS ABDICATED GOVERNMENT HERE, BY DECLARING US OUT OF HIS PROTECTION AND WAGING WAR AGAINST US.

Surely our ruling class is not waging war against us as it was in Colonial America. Or is it?

Those who have lived through the past forty years can see that the War on Poverty is not a war on Poverty . . . . It is a war on poor people.

Those who have lived through the past forty years can see that the War on Drugs is not a war on drugs . . . . It is a war on every person in the U.S. who cannot afford to defend themselves from a system of kangaroo courts.

The so-called "war on drugs" has been the primary excuse our judiciary and lawmakers have used to increase police power to the point where a mere accusation by law enforcement, whether true or untrue, can now result in conviction of a crime and long prison sentences.

With the FBI testifying, falsely in criminal cases, for example, that they can identify someone using a fictional "hair science" technique, no innocent person could possibly avoid being convicted unless they spent hundreds of thousands of dollars in expert witness testimony to overcome the fraudulent perjury of the FBI witnesses.

Even if, by some miracle, an ordinary citizen can find hundreds of thousands of dollars to contradict the FBI "experts," then it is still likely that, because of literal brainwashing from police shows on TV, that the jury would choose to believe the FBI, anyway, in all of the confusion caused by the competing testimony of the experts.

The "war on terrorism" has also become a farce that is nothing more than a war on our civil liberties and freedoms as Americans.

These wars, zealously funded and initiated by the ruling class, are rarely directed against large organizations, such as drug cartels, foreign terrorists or the real factors (such as unemployment) that are driving poverty in the U.S. These wars are mere pretenses for exerting heavy-handed government control over the People of the United States at every possible opportunity.

HERE ARE THE FEDERAL PRISON POPULATION NUMBERS FOR THE PAST FOUR DECADES:

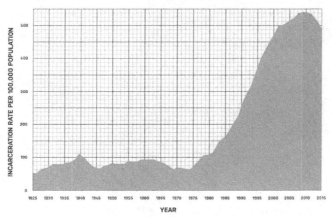

Incarceration rate of inmates under state and federal jurisdiction
per 100,000 population from 1925-2015

Our prisons are full to the brim with poor people and minor drug users. We have a private prison industry thriving from the incarceration of these people (of all races). The private prison industry in the U.S. is one of the largest lobbyists in Washington and in each of the fifty states.

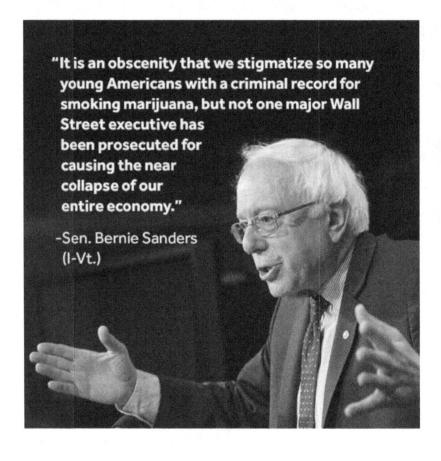

"It is an obscenity that we stigmatize so many young Americans with a criminal record for smoking marijuana, but not one major Wall Street executive has been prosecuted for causing the near collapse of our entire economy."

-Sen. Bernie Sanders (I-Vt.)

XXIV. HE HAS PLUNDERED OUR SEAS, RAV-AGED OUR COASTS, BURNT OUR TOWNS, AND DESTROYED THE LIVES OF OUR PEOPLE.

Surely the ruling class in the U.S. has not plundered the seas, ravaged our Coasts, burnt our town, and destroyed the lives of our people . . . . Have they?

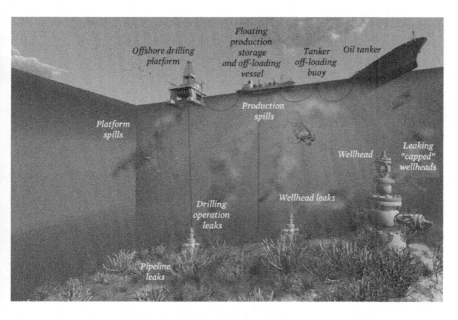

Figure 4 - Courtesy of the Wall Street Journal Has the ruling class plundered our seas? A picture is worth a thousand words:

Time and time again, oil drilling operations, offshore, and oil transportation, have savagely ruined our environments in the U.S. Few invading armies could do as much damage as the environmental catastrophes committed over the past half century in the U.S.

"Those who do not remember history are doomed to repeat it."

Our ruling class ravaging our coastlines? Surely not!

Figure 5 - Dolphins mass exterminated, lying on the Louisiana coastline after the 2010 BP oil disaster.

Has our ruling class burnt our towns? Surely it is only extremism to think or claim that has ever happened in America. Or is it?

In May of 1985, the Philadelphia police department firebombed an entire block of African-American families because one of the homes housed an environmental group.

Figure 6 - Osage Avenue in Philadelphia after police dropped a Tovex bomb on an environmental group. The police prevented the fire department from putting out the fire until the entire block of 60 African-American homes had been burned.

The police used a C-4/Tovex bomb and killed 11 people, including five children. Sixty homes were destroyed.

The incident in Philadelphia was not an isolated incident in America.

Eight years later, Attorney General Janet Reno, because of a personal vendetta against a religious leader, firebombed a civilian complex in Waco, Texas. The result was the death of 76 innocent men, women and children. The ruling class and the corporate controlled media have revised history and paint Janet Reno as a hero.

The atrocities committed by our militarized police force, against our own People, continue to this day. The list of atrocities our militarized police forces have committed against our own People is not a small list.

XXV. HE IS AT THIS TIME TRANSPORTING
LARGE ARMIES OF FOREIGN MERCE-
NARIES TO COMPLEAT THE WORKS OF
DEATH, DESOLATION AND TYRANNY,
ALREADY BEGUN WITH CIRCUM-
STANCES OF CRUELTY & PERFIDY
SCARCELY PARALLELED IN THE MOST
BARBAROUS AGES, AND TOTALLY UN-
WORTHY OF THE HEAD OF A CIVI-
LIZED NATION.

This reference, in the Declaration of Independence, referred to the use of mercenaries
from Austria being used to commit brutalities,
mass murders and intimidation on Colonials.

The modern day parallel to hiring foreign
mercenaries, to terrorize American citizens, lies
in the fact that the militarization of our police
forces is orchestrated by the Israeli military.

The so-called "riots" in Ferguson, Missouri,
in the summer of 2014, were very much a result
of the Ferguson city police department escalating peaceful protests into a military confrontation with ordinary citizens. This unfortunate
escalation of the violence, by the police and the

Governor of the state, was complete with "agent provocateurs" whom the police placed among the peaceful crowds. An *"agent provocateur"* is a person who, at the request of the police, stirs up trouble so that the police have an excuse to use deadly and overwhelming force on peaceful people.

Figure 7 - Actual photo of police deployed to suppress peaceful protestors in Ferguson Missouri who were protesting, ironically, police brutality.

The Israeli military is boastful of its extensive network of influence over U.S. police forces, and their militarization pursuant to Israeli policies.

In their own words:

> *The Law Enforcement Exchange Program (LEEP) was created in cooperation with the Israel National Police, the Israel Ministry of Internal Security, and the Israel Security Agency (Shin Bet) to support and strengthen American law enforcement counter terrorism practices.*[18]

This sounds admirable – i.e. fighting "counter terrorism practices" - until one learns that the Israeli definition of "terrorism" is anyone who protests against the ruling class, or, competes for resources with the ruling class.

The last two reasons in the Declaration of Independence, for secession have been omitted, as they are somewhat rhetorical and repetitive. President Jefferson, reminding us of the fundamentals of Democracy, closes the Declaration of Independence with these words:

> *In every stage of these Oppressions We have Petitioned for Redress in the most humble terms: Our repeated Petitions have been answered only by repeated injury. A Prince whose character is thus marked by every act which may de-*

---

[18] "Empowering Law Enforcement – Protecting America" - Advertising brochure of the Israeli LEEP program.
http://www.jinsa.org/files/LEEPbookletforweb.pdf

fine a Tyrant, is unfit to be the ruler of a free people.

The principles of democracy, well known to President Jefferson, had been founded in a people's revolt in Athens some 2,400 years ago.

DEMOKRATIA

- "Rule by the common people"
- After end of tyranny, nobles contended for power
- An aristocrat named Cleisthenes gained the power of the people by promising radical reforms
- Instead of taking power for himself, gave power to the Assembly (all citizens)
- Poor commoners suddenly had the same rights as nobles

These principles, today, are what Senator Sanders proposes, in his campaign, to restore to the American People from the ruling class that has given cause for a political revolution.

TIME FOR A REVOLUTION

Our Founders understood the meaning of revolution on all levels.

Being enlightened leaders, President Jefferson and President Madison made provisions, in the Constitution, that would insure the ability of the People of the United States to revolt against a tyrannical government.

Unfortunately, at the time of our revolt against Britain, the British had terminated all peaceful means of revolution. Violence became necessary in the revolt of the Colonials against the British, because the ruling class of Britain used military violence to enforce their rule over the colonials.

President Jefferson, however, understood that the best form of revolution is non-violent revolution. President Jefferson understood the need for national defense. However, he viewed passive resistance, and the political process, as the preferred method of overthrowing tyranny.

History has shown that the less violence employed in a revolution, the more likely it is that positive change will result.

One recent change involved a political revolution in California. The voters in California were seriously disenchanted with their existing governor and government system. In 2003, Arnold Schwarzenegger, backed by a huge popular grass roots movement, was able to prevail in a recall election of the elected governor in California. Whether Governor Schwarzenegger was an improvement is subject to debate. What is important, however, is that our political system permitted a peaceful *coup d'état* of the fourth largest economic power in the world. This *coup d'état* was accomplished completely without violence. That is completely unprecedented in history. It is a testament to the genius of our Founders in constructing our political system to permit bloodless revolutions.

Regular elections in our political process provide the same basis for bloodless revolutions. However, history has shown that elections must be backed by a groundswell of supporters, such as those who support Senator Sanders, in order for elections to be effective in creating real change.

It is in this political arena, brilliantly crafted by our Founders, Senator Sanders emerges as a leader of a grass roots political revolution.

In a forty-year political career, that Senator Sanders has frequently been elected to office by the majority of the popular vote. Yet, in those 40 years, he has not waivered in his political observations of the establishment political system in the United States. Senator Sanders has consistently fought for common Americans in his political career. Senator Sanders has consistently fought against special interests to the extent they are detrimental to the average American. There are two reasons why Senator Sanders now leads millions in a political revolution against the corruption and incompetence in our current government.

First, there has been a genuine paradigm shift among voters. Voters have learned that the corporate controlled media is nothing more than a propaganda generator for corporate fascism. Tens of millions of younger voters have been able to see through the corporate dominated media. They realize that the corporate controlled media, in the U.S., is driving a huge campaign of disinformation and misinformation to distract voters with social issues, while, at the same time, persuading voters to endorse special interests that are harmful to the American people themselves.

The second reason Senator Sanders has such broad support is that, unlike any other candidate, Senator Sanders is actually listening to the People of the United States [POTUS]. As Senator Sanders points out to his massive campaign crowds that gather in his support: "This campaign is not about me . . . . It is about **US** (the People)."

Other candidates (of which there are many), are totally oblivious to the thinking of the People of the U.S. They are not only completely out of touch with the thinking of the American People, when they do, rarely, understand what the people are saying, they dismiss it as mere drivel from the peasants. Presidential candidate Jeb Bush once remarked to the press: "The people in this country are angry and frustrated at the establishment and I get that. We have to respect that."

The first clue that he has no intention of respecting the people of the United States is in his comment. He demeans the concerns of Americans as being merely irrational emotional reactions, rather than as being the well-supported concerns that Americans have over corruption and incompetence in our government.

Americans, however, have come to understand that supporting establishment politicians, such as Bush, is the same as perpetuating a ruling elite comprised of wealthy individuals and multinational corporations. Americans are finally beginning to understand that the ruling elite in the U.S. will ruthlessly drain our economy, exploit our environment, perpetuate infinite war, and impose austerity on the American people to pay for it. American voters finally understand that the ruling elite literally "owns" the establishment candidates. Americans finally understand that the ruling elite will not create jobs, or invest in America and Americans. Much of this paradigm shift has resulted from social media. Social media provides a means for Americans to exchange information that is, literally, willfully suppressed in the corporate controlled mainstream media.

For 40 years, Orwellian slogans such as "law and order," "trickle down economics," "protect and serve," "Patriot Act," "Freedom of Information," "transparent government," and thousands of others, have finally become visible to the public as mere manipulative deceptions.

Laws that are supposedly designed to protect people abound. Those laws, however, are usually applied in such a manner that they usually work against the common man, and, favor only the wealthy who are in control of resources and government power in the U.S.

The result is that the entire legal and judicial system in the U. S. has been perverted to serve a ruling class of billionaires, and their political puppets, who view the American people as their own private property. An analogy for this is "slavery."

This slavery has been progressively imposed on the American people subtly, in small increments, over a period of 40 years. Most Americans didn't realize what was happening. Corporate media had convinced hundreds of millions of people that the strife, economic difficulties, and problems in the world were a product of the defects in the American people (such as sexism, racism, refusal to work, improper personal financial management, choices to eschew education, refusing to accept personal responsibility, etc., etc., etc.).

What Americans have come to understand, however, and what Senator Sanders has understood for 40 years, is that our system is "rigged" so that the American people cannot succeed except in service of the greed of the ruling class.

The billionaire ruling class in America, by using a small fraction of their wealth, now control the government, and a fascist army of police, to insure that the system remains rigged. Americans are, only now, by being able to exchange individual perspectives and views in social media, able to shift their understanding of how the system is rigged against them.

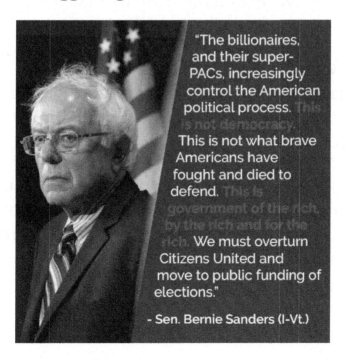

"The billionaires, and their super-PACs, increasingly control the American political process. This is not democracy. This is not what brave Americans have fought and died to defend. This is government of the rich, by the rich and for the rich. We must overturn Citizens United and move to public funding of elections."

- Sen. Bernie Sanders (I-Vt.)

This paradigm shift, in the perceptions of the American People, seems to have arisen from a collective consciousness. It is as if the American People have finally acquired the critical thinking skills to evaluate the relentless propaganda of the mainstream corporate media. They are applying those same critical thinking skills to re-evaluating the government policies of the past 40 years. These are the same policies of the last forty years that have led to the elimination of the American middle class, and resulted in the metaphorical enslavement of our own People.

But there is more to this revolution than the identification of antagonists in the corporate controlled government, and the corporate controlled media.

As one takes a look around America, at other Americans, as a People we are achieving an enlightenment not seen before in our mainstream culture.

Even as we identify the many problems in our culture, in our government, in our economy and in our daily lives, Americans are beginning to awaken to a new sense of compassion for humanity, and, those helpless and less fortunate among us.

More and more, the People of the United States are understanding that condemning others, kicking down doors, and hurting each other, is not a solution to the problems we are trying to solve.

More and more the POTUS are understanding, and applying, the enlightened realization that our government, and the ruling class, has no right to punish Americans, interminably, just because they made a wrong choice at some point in their lives.

Senator Sanders is speaking, eloquently, to this new American enlightenment. In his agendas, Senator Sanders frequently proposes pathways for people to come back from improvident decisions in their lives. This is the essence of this revolution – the creation of new pathways for Americans to adjust to an ever changing world that is growing smaller, and smaller, and smaller each day.

In terms of those imprisoned, Senator Sanders proposes that we MUST have laws that insure those discharged from a prison have employment, some education, the means to fend for themselves in an economy hostile to workers, and the means to provide for their basic necessities such as housing and medical care.

In terms of undocumented or "illegal" aliens, Senator Sanders proposes that there be a regulated pathway towards citizenship. This would recognize the fact that nothing we do is likely to stop the flow of immigrants to the United States. Indeed, we may have moral imperatives not to stop the flow of immigrants.

President John F. Kennedy, in this book "A Nation of Immigrants" has persuasively pointed out that America was founded upon the risk taking, toil and devotion of immigrants from its very inception. In the history of the United States, immigrants, and immigration, has been our greatest strength.

Immigration from all points of the earth was a premise upon which the Founders built our great Constitution and political process.

Just as the Romans ruled over a vast empire of diverse cultures, geographies, demographics, economics, trade, religions and social structures, our Founders implemented the *Ius Genitum (governance of the people, by the people and for the people)* of ancient Rome to provide a system of law and government for vast diversities of people.[19]   A pathway to citizenship would be an alternative to arresting all illegals (undocumented aliens) and deporting them.   It would provide a means of giving them living wages that do not suppress the wages of other workers in the U.S. It would allow 11 million people to meaningfully participate in the future of this Country, and, its restoration to a leader of democracy and freedom in the World.

Alternative pathways, such as this, that are respectful of the rights of People to equality, dignity and self-actualization, are signatures of the campaign of Senator Sanders.

Perhaps that is why there are so many People willing to join him in a political revolution.

"Comes the time, comes the Man."[20]

---

[19]   Maine, Henry Sumner, ANCIENT LAW, Cambridge (1864).

[20] Attributed to Shakespeare as the author of "St. Thomas More." Shakespeare's identity as the author of various works is sometimes obscure in history. Shakespeare as a Catholic was subject to summary execution by Queen Elizabeth for his religious beliefs.

BERNIE'S PLATFORM

- UNIVERSAL HEALTH CARE
- FREE/AFFORDABLE PUBLIC COLLEGE
- TRANSFORM OUR ENERGY SYSTEM
- OVERTURN CITIZENS UNITED
- RAISE THE MINIMUM WAGE TO $15
- END THE WAR ON DRUGS
- REBUILD OUR CRUMBLING INFRASTRUCTURE
- RAISE TAXES ON THE 1%
- STOP ENDLESS MILITARY SPENDING
- EXPAND SOCIAL SECURITY
- END POLICE BRUTALITY
- DEMILITARIZE THE POLICE

UNIVERSAL HEALTH CARE

As our global economy expands, spurred by transportation and telecommunications technology, the U.S. has fallen behind with the changes in other developed countries.

Healthcare Spending as % GDP

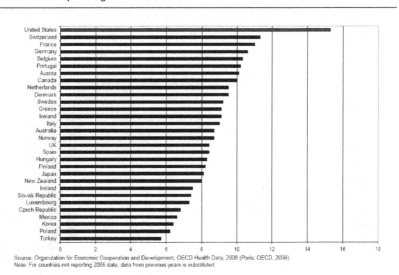

Source: Organization for Economic Cooperation and Development, OECD Health Data, 2008 (Paris: OECD, 2008).
Note: For countries not reporting 2006 data, data from previous years is substituted.

Healthcare in the U.S., as of 2014, accounts

for the expenditure of 17.4% of our GDP and it is likely to increase each year with our aging populations. Americans spend more in healthcare, *per capita*, than any other Nation in the world.

Notwithstanding this incredible expenditure of economic resources on healthcare, the United States remains one of the least favorable countries for healthcare among first world countries.

The American "health" system, outrageously, bears a resemblance to the health system that existed in the former Soviet Union when it collapsed.

America's system is an unnecessarily complex system in which Insurance companies, and corporate administrators, double the cost of health care, by taking profits out of the system, at the expense of health care professionals, healthcare workers, patients and the general public.

Our current system "evolved" during the Reagan area when de-regulation became a focus of worship in our political system.

The de-regulation of industries in the U.S. insured maximum profits for corporate administrators, shareholders and insurance companies, while at the same time vastly reducing the competence, efficiency and effectiveness of the overall system of healthcare in the U.S. The days of the benevolent physician, who could do his or her best for those under their care, are over. The system became driven not by the care and concern of the health professionals, but, became driven purely by profits.

This profit worship, naturally, invited a concept from the former Soviet Union known as "capitated health care."

In the old Former Soviet Union [FSU], health care costs were managed by allocating a specific amount of money to each city, town or region. When the physicians had spent all the money (which was typically about 10% of what was actually needed for quality health care), no more money, medical resources or treatments were available to the people within a specific geographic limitation. Physicians and healthcare professionals were forced to impose healthcare "austerity" on those seeking medical care when their allotted resources "ran out."

Private insurance companies in the U.S. now routinely employ capitated health coverage. This is most evident in "Health Maintenance Organizations" or "HMO's." The HMO pretends that it can deliver quality health care at a lower cost than regular insurance companies. What actually happens, however, is that the HMO gives a specific, very limited amount of money to a primary care physician to care for his pool of HMO patients. If the physician reduces the amount of care he gives to the patients in his pool, then, he may keep the excess. If he exceeds the costs the HMO has allocated to his patient pool, then, he must make up the difference out of his own pocket. The entire purpose of this Soviet inspired scheme is to shift the full risk of medical insurance to doctors, and healthcare facilities, and relieve the insurance companies (or government) of risk so that they can be assured of high profits.

In the FSU [Former Soviet Union], in which capitated healthcare originated, the system degenerated to the point in which few people, unless they paid cash to the physicians and nurses, were actually able to obtain the healthcare they needed. For example, a physician may be permitted to only take three x-rays a day. If he had to see 11 emergencies requiring x-rays, then, he would simply have to treat 8 of the patients without taking x-rays. If a patient was authorized a hospital stay, because the nurses and nurse assistants were so poorly paid, they would not give baths, change bedpans, or change bed linens unless the patient paid them directly, in cash (and usually in U.S. dollars). It was not unusual for surgeons to run out of their daily allotment of anesthetic during surgery. The patients were simply restrained on the operating table until the surgery was finished (screams and struggles of the patient notwithstanding) because the surgeon had exceeded his allotment of anesthetics. More anesthesia was available if the patient's family chose to pay the surgeon, extra, for the "extra" anesthetic.

The theory that this system of organized crime uses to justify itself is that the primary care physician, as a "cost gatekeeper," will minimize the amount of unnecessary care in the system. However, what really happens, is that the HMO's pocket huge profits, by only allocating a small amount of the money they collect from premiums, to the actual care of the patient. There is virtually no effective regulation of this system of organized crime.

Senator Sanders points out that virtually all first-world nations, except the U.S., currently have a "single payer" system of healthcare. In simple terms, a "single payer" system is a system of healthcare in which the administrators of the healthcare do not have a profit motive. In addition, under a "single payer" system of healthcare, all of the health care professionals and providers are governed by the same set of rules. Under a uniform system of rules, and, interpretation of those rules, it is far more likely that waste in the healthcare system is going to be minimized rather than under a chaotic system of individual insurers, and, profit motivated administrators who impose "austerity" in the system on the most vulnerable and needy in the system.

Such a system, "Medicare," has successfully operated in the U.S. for well over half of a century. Polls show that the majority of Americans support the expansion of "Obamacare" into a nationwide, single payer system that would be administered under the regulatory and supervisory umbrella of Medicare.

As with most of Senator Sanders' agenda items, the concept of a single payer healthcare system interfaces with other items on the agenda. One of the most crucial aspects of an improved healthcare system for the United States includes an adequately compensated workforce that has proper rewards for extending care, especially to our aging population.

Nurses are widely and chronically underpaid in our system of healthcare. The same is true of many nurses aids and others directly involved in the moment-to-moment, day to day medical care of Americans. These "frontline" workers should receive the compensation that is now being wasted on the profit managers of insurance companies, and wasted on administrators who are highly paid to suppress the wages of healthcare workers.

AFFORDABLE PUBLIC COLLEGES:
Reforming Education

The concept of College as a means of advancing in life, and, as a means of movement through social/economic strata, led to an extraordinary transformation of our higher education system in the last half of the Twentieth Century.

After World War II, the wide availability of the G.I. Bill allowed many middle class Americans to attend college who might otherwise not have had the opportunity. This body of educated Americans were successful, individually, and were also successful as a collective in bringing the U.S. into the electronic age, and, the general prosperity that prevailed in the U.S. up until the 1980's [the Reagan era].

Educators, politicians, sociologists and others in our culture made the observation that individuals succeeded, and contributed greatly to our economy and world status, if they had college educations. These groups of observers then made a giant leap in logic in jumping to the conclusion that a college education, alone, is sufficient to provide individuals with social and economic mobility.

A college degree is a requirement in U.S. culture for advancing in the job market. A college degree, however, without more, is no guarantee in U.S. culture of social or economic mobility. A college degree is nothing more than a "lottery ticket" that enables a graduate to compete with approximately 20 other graduates for available jobs requiring education in a particular field.

This is designed to serve corporate interests. Large multinational corporations, and economic collectives, have their pick of massive amounts of graduates. Only about 1 in 20, however, will ever find the type of job of which they are dreaming when they attend colleges and universities. This has resulted in massive unemployment among "milenials" who are just graduating from college and entering the job market.

Persons from outside the U.S. currently observe that our education system is not really educating its students. It is merely preparing them to compete for jobs, as workers for corporations (or, alternatively, for government positions).

The Great Generation that weathered the depression, and fought World War II, had succeeded as an educated generation, not just because
its leaders graduated from colleges and universities. The Great Generation also succeeded because a strong labor movement, and a strong
economy provided jobs for them in which they
could apply their education for the general
prosperity of America. That generation also
succeeded because of what they were required
to study in order to achieve a degree.

In the rush to mass produce "educated"
workers after the 1970's; our college system
abandoned the core elements of an education.
Those core elements included a degree candidate's ability to use the scientific method. Another core element of an education that was
abandoned by our "modern" system, was the requirement that degree candidates be able to go
directly to the source of great minds and directly
interpret what those great minds had given us
in terms of enlightenment. Instead, our education system "dumbed" down our method of intellectual inquiry so that students are only required to regurgitate popular derivatives of what
great minds had given us, instead of having to
understand what the great minds had provided

to us themselves. Students are never taught to think for themselves. Quite the opposite, students are now conditioned to accept only the "politically correct" views of their teachers and administrators.

No longer are students required to study Aristotle, or his extraordinary treatises on logic and logical fallacies. The result is that most students graduating from college are incapable of critical thinking. They have been trained only to understand what it is that someone else believes, and to express that belief to the person who believes it.

The result of this is that many (most) "educated" Americans lack the fundamental cognitive skills necessary for an informed electorate.

With the "dumbing down" of Americans, through a poor (but mandatory) system of education, the corporate media has found it easy to divide and manipulate voters. Voter decisions no longer turn on informed evaluation of facts. Voter decisions turn upon slogans, popularity of candidates, blind political ideologies (e.g. conservative vs. liberal), corporate propaganda, and the will of the ruling elite.

Mathematics — 55.4%

Mean score	Country
613	Shanghai-China
573	Singapore
560	Chinese Taipei
561	Hong Kong-China
554	Korea
535	Liechtenstein
538	Macao-China
536	Japan
531	Switzerland
515	Belgium
523	Netherlands
514	Germany
518	Poland
518	Canada
519	Finland
500	New Zealand
504	Australia
521	Estonia
506	Austria
501	Slovenia
511	Viet Nam
495	France
499	Czech Republic
494	OECD average
494	United Kingdom
490	Luxembourg
493	Iceland
482	Slovak Republic
501	Ireland
487	Portugal
500	Denmark
485	Italy
489	Norway
466	Israel
477	Hungary
481	United States

Reading

Mean score	Country
570	Shanghai-China
542	Singapore
538	Japan
545	Hong Kong-China
536	Korea
512	New Zealand
524	Finland
505	France
523	Canada
509	Belgium
523	Chinese Taipei
512	Australia
523	Ireland
516	Liechtenstein
504	Norway
518	Poland
511	Netherlands
486	Israel
509	Switzerland
508	Germany
488	Luxembourg
499	United Kingdom
496	OECD average
516	Estonia
498	United States
483	Sweden
509	Macao-China
490	Italy
493	Czech Republic
483	Iceland
488	Portugal
488	Hungary
488	Spain
490	Austria
496	Denmark
477	Greece

Science

Mean score	Country
580	Shanghai-China
551	Singapore
547	Japan
545	Finland
555	Hong Kong-China
521	Australia
516	New Zealand
541	Estonia
524	Germany
522	Netherlands
538	Korea
525	Canada
514	United Kingdom
526	Poland
522	Ireland
525	Liechtenstein
514	Slovenia
515	Switzerland
505	Belgium
501	OECD average
523	Chinese Taipei
491	Luxembourg
528	Viet Nam
499	France
506	Austria
508	Czech Republic
495	Norway
497	United States
498	Denmark
521	Macao-China
485	Sweden
494	Italy
494	Hungary
470	Israel
478	Iceland
496	Lithuania

Figure 8 - Notwithstanding the fact that the U.S. is near the top in spending money, our education performance ranks near the bottom of developed countries. Courtesy of "Business Insider."

Notwithstanding the "dumbing down" of America, including the "dumbing down" of its higher education system, college is still a prerequisite for advancement through social and economic strata.

For that reason, Senator Sanders is proposing in his platform that college once again be affordable to all persons in the U.S.

Affordability is the issue because it would give all Americans an equal chance to compete in the job market (once our economy again begins producing jobs).

In the past thirty years, universities and colleges have become profit centers for special interests. College administrators are paid enormous sums of compensation to use their corporate, and familial, connections in developing the reputation of universities and colleges. The result of this, however, is that private endowments of colleges and universities come with strings attached. This has resulted in an enormous rise in the cost of tuition at not only private universities, but public universities as well. Seeking money, influence and profits, these universities place an emphasis on extra-curriculars, such as sports, research and political agendas. The education of students has become secondary.

In addition, universities and colleges now exist mostly for the benefit of administrators and benefactors as opposed to the students who attend them. Consequently, the students are viewed as a profit pool to increase the moneyed influence of those in privilege within the academic structure.

While Wall Street investment banks, and

TBTF ["Too Big to Fail Banks"] received a massive bailout from the taxpayers, and years of no interest loans from the Federal Reserve, the U.S. government now charges students 8-10% interest, per year, on student loans. The result is that students graduating from college have a lifetime of debt shackled to them that is often on the magnitude of a house mortgage. With this debt, they then only have about a 1 in 20 chance of obtaining a job that will provide a salary sufficient to service the education debt, support a family, own a home and have the modest enjoyment of a middle class disposable income.

The American dream is dead (except for children of the privileged ruling elite).

Senator Sanders' answer to this is to propose legislation that would (a) soften the impact of existing student loans on college graduates seeking employment in the workforce; and (b) require all public colleges and universities to provide free tuition (and seek profits from some source other than students).

Senator Sanders' platform proposes to impose a transaction tax on Wall Street speculation in order to pay for this system of free tuition. What Senator Sanders proposes is a ½ of one percent tax on speculative transactions. The justification for this tax is to reimburse the U.S. taxpayers for the costs, (and personal sacrifices of the American People), for the 2008 bailout of Wall Street, and, the bloated monopolistic system of TBTF banks that have arisen in this country.

Senator Sanders' proposed law, known as "The College for All Act" also would impose very modest transaction taxes on Bonds (0.1% fee) and a 0.005% tax on derivatives.[21]

Important aspects of Senator Sanders' proposal is that graduates with debts would be permitted to re-finance their student debt if the current interest rates on student debts are lowered. The law also would lower existing interest rates on student loans from 4.32% to 2.32% to more fairly and accurately reflect current interest rates.

The law would also streamline the application process for financial aid. Senator Sanders proposes that students would not have to re-apply for financial aid each year, but, simply update their initial application. This idea, and removing barriers to applications of low-income students, would significantly enhance the ability of low-income students to participate in financial aid and ultimately achieve a college education.

Finally, the law would provide for an expanded, ad well-funded student work program. The program would specifically target colleges and

---

[21] A derivative is simply a contract to trade in the profit or losses of other securities (such as stocks and bonds), or, in the debts held by investors, or in other forms of assets such as foreign currencies.

universities that have low-income students.

Admittedly, this plan by Senator Sanders would not guarantee an improvement in our system of education.

There is something very important, however, that it *would* accomplish.

Right now, the risk of getting an education that might not be marketable is entirely on the individual. This law would shift that risk, appropriately, to the businesses that profit the most from a well-educated pool of potential workers. This Bill places most of the cost of a college education on businesses that are supposed to be creating jobs. It is only fair that the ruling elite pay for their "pool" of educated workers, in exchange for the ruling elite's use of our infrastructure, and workers, to create their wealth.

TRANSFORMING OUR ENERGY

In 1992, Daniel Yergen, in a Pulitzer Prize winning book, pointed out that our species could now be described as "hydrocarbon man."

In "The Prize: The Epic Quest for Oil, Money & Power"[22] Mr. Yergen presents an exhaustive history of the use and development of hydrocarbon fuels in our civilization up to modern day.

Civilization has had energy driven technologies, contrary to popular belief, for thousands of years. The technology included the ancient Romans' use of siphons and gravity to transport water over great distances to where it was required in cities. Using no electrical or motive power, the Romans provided more fresh water to the ancient city of Rome than we currently provide to the borough of Manhattan. Ancient Greeks used waterpower to cut massive blocks of stone for their architecture. The same may also have been true of ancient Egyptians in their

---

[22] Yergin, Daniel, THE PRIZE: THE EPIC QUEST FOR OIL, MONEY & POWER, Free Press, New York, rev'd. ed. (2008).

construction of the pyramids, and, their massive masonry cities.

The ancient Greeks had also developed some technologies that we would consider technologically advanced even in our own day. Archimedes, for instance, hundreds of years before the Christian era, had developed rudimentary steam engines, solar concentrators, navigation computers, vending machines and robots.

When Europe began emerging from the dark ages, and education became more available in Europe and other parts of the world, scholars re-discovered the ancient Arabic, Greek and Roman works that are the foundations of modern mathematics and science. Fluency in both ancient Greek and Latin became a pre-requisite to achieving a university education. This widespread revival of the ancient languages allowed many brilliant people to study the ancients, in their original language, and glean information and learning from original manuscripts to which they added their own brilliant insights.

The people who studied the ancients went on to create modern chemistry, mathematics (including the Calculus), astronomy, metallurgy, physics, fluid and dynamic engineering, and all of the other scientific advancements credited to

humanity in our own age. The people who studied the ancients in their own languages also
created the architecture for our great Constitution.

Our own Founders were principally educated
in the classics of ancient Greece and Rome. At
the time of the American Revolution, the meaning of having an education meant that one was
fluent in Latin and Greek, and, had read, in the
original languages of the great ancient minds.
President Thomas Jefferson once remarked on
the value of an education based upon the Classics: "A third value is in the stores of real science deposited and transmitted us in these languages, to-wit: in history, ethics, arithmetic, ge-
ometry, astronomy, and natural history."

From this Classic revival, new advancements
in chemistry led to the field of metallurgy and
the development of steel production methods.
For the first time in history, man began to build
and innovate with materials that could with-
stand the pressures of steam, and, harness its
energy value. Toward the later part of the Nineteenth century, with the development of the internal combustion engine, man had developed a
means of exploiting hydrocarbons that had

stored energy in the ground for millions of years.

The study of the Classics led to the re-invention of the steam engine. The steam engine allowed for the development of railroads. For the first time in history, humanity had a means of economically transporting huge amounts of iron ore, and coal for furnaces, to a central location.

Advances in chemistry and metallurgy allowed for the development of mass production of steel (especially high carbon steel). This gave humanity a universal, relatively lightweight and strong, means of building structures.

At this point in history, however, because of the businesses monopolies of the late nineteenth century, the immense profitability of those monopolies, in the U.S. and Europe, stifled further developments in the industrial development of transportation, heating and building technology. The age of the "Robber Barons" had arrived.

Rather than making modest sums of money from rendering coal, steel, railroads, electricity production and construction more cost-efficient, or eco-friendly, the Robber Barons used manipulative and deceitful business techniques to stifle all competition, and, render the public fully dependent upon their profit gorging monopolies. This dependence on hydrocarbon energy sources, and hydrocarbon markets, persists today in the U.S. and around the world.

This is not irrelevant history. The ruling class in America has used the exact same tactics, as the Robber Barons, to rig our economic and political system exactly as it was rigged prior to the Great Depression.

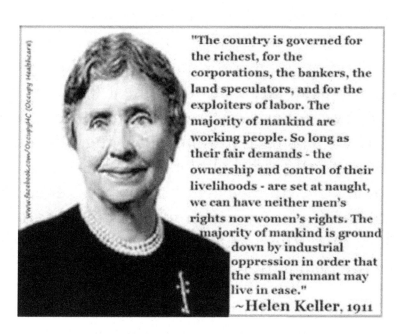

"The country is governed for the richest, for the corporations, the bankers, the land speculators, and for the exploiters of labor. The majority of mankind are working people. So long as their fair demands - the ownership and control of their livelihoods - are set at naught, we can have neither men's rights nor women's rights. The majority of mankind is ground down by industrial oppression in order that the small remnant may live in ease."
~Helen Keller, 1911

Andrew Carnegie used private armies of "Pinkertons" to forcefully suppress dissent among the working class, just as the ruling class, today, uses 1.2M taxpayer funded police. Heavy policing makes certain that the middle and lower classes cannot demonstrate effectively, or strike for better wages. The workers in Carnegie's factories were dying from high rates of industrial accidents because of exhaustion on the job from endless workweeks and low starvation wages.

Similarly, today, Americans are working more hours, and more minimum wage jobs than they have ever worked in their recent history. Our workforce is exhausted and the industrial death and accident rate among male dominated jobs, in particular, is at its highest levels in half a century. Americans are working harder, and longer, for less of a standard of living, than they have since the time of the Robber Barons. In addition, the ruling class has so weakened the social safety net for which workers fought in the 1930's, that the industrial accident and death rates are decimating working families.

This is an intentional scheme by those who control multi-national corporations, just as it was intentional by the Robber Barons in the end of the nineteenth century. By keeping the majority of workers impoverished (instead of well-paid and supported with benefits) the large multi-nationals in the U.S. profit, greatly, just as the Robber Barons profited from an impoverished America. If the working class, and the middle class of America, are at marginally starvation levels, then they have few choices but to submit to the profit generating schemes for large multi-national corporations and the ruling elite.

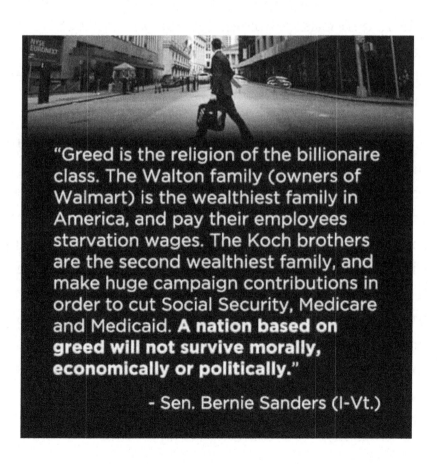

"Greed is the religion of the billionaire class. The Walton family (owners of Walmart) is the wealthiest family in America, and pay their employees starvation wages. The Koch brothers are the second wealthiest family, and make huge campaign contributions in order to cut Social Security, Medicare and Medicaid. **A nation based on greed will not survive morally, economically or politically.**"

- Sen. Bernie Sanders (I-Vt.)

Walmart is a good example. With Americans making less and less in the past forty years, and, with their earning power and savings being consumed by inflation, Americans have no choice but to patronize businesses, such as Walmart, which sell cheap, substandard products, most of which are made overseas by workers earning $0.54 per hour or less. American wages are so low that American workers can only afford cheap imported goods. Companies like Walmart, which have invested billions in Chinese manufacturers, and which exploit Chinese labor, can dump foreign goods on the U.S. market, indefinitely, at artificially low prices, to exclude competition from any U.S. Manufacturers and retailers.

Overall, Americans do not benefit from companies like Walmart. Although lower prices seem appealing, "there is no free lunch." Americans pay an incredible cost for Walmart's dumping of Chinese goods on the American market. First, Walmart (the largest employer in the U.S.), by paying disgustingly low wages, and no benefits, creates a class of workers who are dependent on government subsidies such as Medicaid, food stamps, welfare, etc. Walmart is also placing an incredible strain on our nation's infrastructure. Walmart uses our roads, our telecommunications networks, our sewer and trash systems, our landfills, our ports, our workforce services, our unemployment tax reserves, and thousands of other aspects of our complex economy and infrastructure.

The same is true of our multinational oil companies. Americans have no choice but to drive gasoline consuming vehicles because car manufacturers and oil companies will not develop alternate sources of transportation for ordinary Americans, and, they actively try to destroy anyone who offers competition to gas consuming vehicles.

The fact is that science provided us with alternatives to hydrocarbon energy sources, and, gasoline fueled cars, very early in the twentieth century. However, the oil companies have become so wealthy, that they are, at a relatively small cost of corrupting our own government, capable of suppressing any meaningful alternatives to huge amounts of gasoline consumption.

The unwritten and unspoken trusts between big oil and big auto manufacturers insure that cars will burn gasoline, instead of using electricity or fuel cells.

In the same way, the robber barons had created monopolies in the late nineteenth century. Rockefeller, for example, used deceit, bribery and manipulation to create a monopoly in the petroleum industry. Carmakers were given little choice but to develop cars that ran on gasoline rather than on electricity. Rockefeller, with his vast fortune, just like the robber barons of today (the ruling elite) litigated competitors out of business. The competitors to oil that he ruined, by using his legal influence over the courts, included Nikolas Tesla and Westinghouse. Nikolas Tesla and Westinghouse, with their innovations, could have provided most of our electricity needs for the next century from hydroelectric power, or solar power, or wind power, or tidal current power, instead of coal-fueled power plants. Tesla and Westinghouse, if they had not been ruined by the moneyed corruption of the courts, from litigation by J.P. Morgan and General Electric, would have developed efficient, and affordable, clean energy electric cars a hundred years ago.

The result is that we have billions of automobiles, everyday, consuming huge amounts of petroleum and converting that petroleum into poisons, such as carbon monoxide, that are becoming a toxic factor in our atmosphere. This has not changed over the past 125 years, in large measure, because of the huge amount of wealth concentrated in multi-national oil companies. They are able to use that massive wealth to corrupt our own government, and, the governments of other countries, to perpetuate their monopoly on the transportation available to ordinary people. Ordinary people have no realistic choices but to rely upon gasoline driven vehicles in order to compete in the workforce for transportation to and from work.

The result is tens of millions of tons of poisons, such as carbon monoxide, being poured into Earth's atmosphere on a daily basis by hundreds of millions of cars and hydrocarbon emitting plants worldwide. Coal burning power plants are discharging a similar amount of carbon contaminants, along with other poisons such as sulfur and mercury.

For over forty years, scientists have been collecting empirical evidence and data. Almost unanimously scientists have discovered, and confirmed, that these large imbalances of contaminants in the atmosphere are responsible for serious changes in weather patterns.

The only dissenters to this scientific hypothesis are the industries that are making tens of billions of dollars perpetrating the discharge of the hydrocarbon contaminants.

The most frightening aspect of this global climate change, due to hydrocarbon emissions, is that we do not know if it can be reversed. We *do* know, however, that those who profit from carbon emissions are imposing a tremendous cost on humanity. Those costs come in the form of increased health care (especially for those residing in large metropolitan areas), the costs of the military for keeping peace in regions where we draw foreign reserves of petroleum, scientific research to correct the problem, and many other burdens caused by excessive (and avoidable) carbon emissions.

Perhaps the greatest cost imposed on humanity from the profits of carbon emission industries, is the fact that the more profit these industries made for their owners, the more it stifles the development of alternate sources of energy which can avoid carbon emissions.

Senator Sanders' approach includes, first, to tax carbon emissions. Unfortunately, for forty years, Congress has been trying, unsuccessfully, to pass legislation that would require carbon emission industries to pay for the damage they are doing to the United States and the People of the United States. The profits in hydrocarbon industries are so immense, and, the ability of those profits to corrupt Congress is as equally immense, that no one has yet been able to pass any meaningful legislation to deter the hydrocarbon industries from their accelerating influence on climate change.

In Senator Sanders' realization of a political revolution in the U.S., it becomes a number one priority for voters to remove Congressional members who have historically sheltered and protected the hydrocarbon industries from effective regulation. We must replace those representatives with lawmakers who will impose responsibility for the damage ruling elite profiteering is inflicting on the rest of humanity.

One of Senator Sanders' other approaches has been to lead the fight against further dependence on hydrocarbon fuels. This effort by Senator Sanders includes his staunch opposition to the Keystone pipeline.

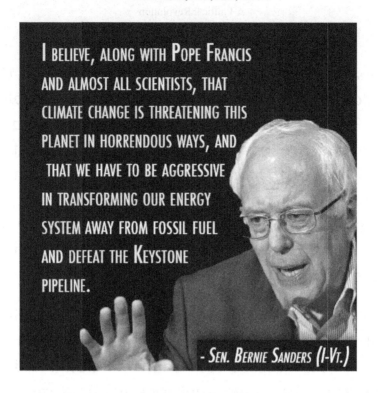

I BELIEVE, ALONG WITH POPE FRANCIS AND ALMOST ALL SCIENTISTS, THAT CLIMATE CHANGE IS THREATENING THIS PLANET IN HORRENDOUS WAYS, AND THAT WE HAVE TO BE AGGRESSIVE IN TRANSFORMING OUR ENERGY SYSTEM AWAY FROM FOSSIL FUEL AND DEFEAT THE KEYSTONE PIPELINE.

- SEN. BERNIE SANDERS (I-VT.)

The Keystone pipeline is a huge gift to multi-national petroleum corporations. It is also a huge facilitator of perpetuating petroleum based hydrocarbon emissions into the atmosphere.

The Keystone pipeline is designed to carry heavy amounts of soil-contaminated oil from Canada to ports in Houston Texas. Although the pipeline would marginally increase the global pool of oil, there would be almost no economic benefits to the U.S. The pipeline would, in fact, cause the U.S. to become a means of perpetuating China's incredibly high carbon emission rate. Most of the oil that would be shipped from Canada to Texas would be exported and shipped to China. China would benefit immensely from cheap oil, yet China is now the largest carbon polluter on the planet. The U.S. would bear the ecological disasters from leaks in the pipeline (which are almost inevitable as the pipeline traverses numerous geo-active areas in the Central U.S.). In addition, the pipeline would traverse the single largest underground aquifer (water supply) in the United States.

This pipeline would, indefinitely, extend the profit incentives for multinational oil companies to continue development of hydrocarbon based technologies, for transportation and power generation, long beyond the point when they could be replaced with alternative energy technology such as solar, wind technology and hydrogen fuel cell technology.

Senator Sanders has led the fight, in Congress, against the Keystone pipeline. In addition, he has also led the fight in Congress to provide funding for development and deployment of alternate energy production sources. These alternate energy production sources would be renewable, non-consumptive, and would eliminate carbon emissions for most energy applications in the U.S.

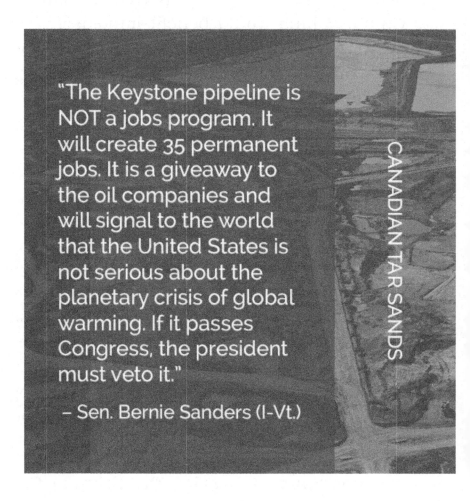

"The Keystone pipeline is NOT a jobs program. It will create 35 permanent jobs. It is a giveaway to the oil companies and will signal to the world that the United States is not serious about the planetary crisis of global warming. If it passes Congress, the president must veto it."

– Sen. Bernie Sanders (I-Vt.)

CANADIAN TAR SANDS

OVERTURN CITIZENS UNITED:

Citizens United refers to a decision of the United States Supreme Court,[23] effectively denying Congress the authority to outlaw bribery of public officials in the United States.

Defenders of the decision (mostly wealthy individuals, entrenched politicians and multinational corporations) view the decision as granting "equal rights" to the wealthy to exercise First Amendment rights of free speech, and lobbying.

A reading of the Court's (tortured) opinion, and its scathing dissent, shows that the U.S. Supreme Court has been bought, and paid for, by the wealthy powers that arranged for the appointment of conservative justices.

The real issue was: "Can political interests use large sums of money, to take over the national mass media, to brainwash the public for or against a particular candidate." The Su-

---

[23] *Citizens United v. Federal Election Comm.*, 558 U.S. 310 (2010)

preme Court majority responded: "No problem."

Over the past forty years, since the Reagan presidency, the ruling class has seated numerous representatives and senators in Congress who made certain that taxes would be lowered on the ruling class. The promises those representatives made were that the ruling class would use the extra money to create jobs and stimulate the economy. In fact, the exact opposite happened.

The ruling class took a substantial part of the tax breaks they received, and used those profits to elect even more representatives who were completely loyal only to the ruling elite. The money was used to buy immense amounts of mass media advertising to perpetuate the power and profit of the ruling class. History would show that almost none of the tax breaks went to the creation of jobs or improving the U.S. economy. None of the money was used to develop alternate forms of energy. Much of the money was used to divert us to an outrageously costly war in the Middle-East, for which the wealthy have not yet paid, that did nothing but increase the profits of those involved in conducting the war.

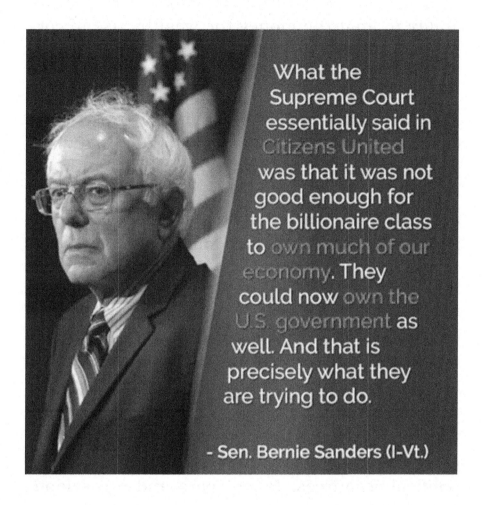

What the Supreme Court essentially said in Citizens United was that it was not good enough for the billionaire class to own much of our economy. They could now own the U.S. government as well. And that is precisely what they are trying to do.

- Sen. Bernie Sanders (I-Vt.)

The effect of the Citizen's United decision is that Congress is prohibited from passing laws that can limit the "favors" that wealthy people can perform, with their disposable wealth, for OUR representatives.

The real result is that the average person, who has little or no wealth to influence legislators, judges or government employees, has no ability to limit the money the wealthy use to corrupt the government into serving the wealthy and the ruling elite instead of the people.

A family, struggling to pay for the necessities of life, could never hope, even if they band together with other families, to raise enough money to match the contributions profit making elite are willing to make to politicians in order to corrupt and control our government.

Given our current views on Supreme Court rulings, there are only two ways to reverse this court-sponsored corruption of the U. S. Government. The first would be a constitutional amendment holding that showering politicians with money and favors is not "protected speech" under the First Amendment. Unfortunately, constitutional amendments require extensive political resources, takes years and are seldom successful. The second method is for the Supreme Court to overrule its decision to support corruption of the federal government.

Senator Sanders has assured the public, that if elected President, he will appoint no one to the Supreme Court, during his term, unless that appointee passes the "litmus test" of promising to vote for overturning Citizens' United.

RAISE THE MINIMUM WAGE TO $15

Few initiatives carry more superstitions, misconceptions, and fears, than raising the minimum wage.

The conservative arguments against raising the minimum wage are that it will cause employers to hire less people, cause inflation, drive businesses out of business, and a host of moral arguments. Often, one of those "moral arguments" is that common people do not deserve any more than a small amount for the work and services they provide to the U.S. economy.

There are, however, many arguments based on sound economic principles that mandate a raise of the minimum wage in the U.S. The arguments for raising the minimum wage make sense, mostly, if we lose the outdated economic views of the 1940's in favor of an intelligent analysis of todays corrupt economy. The economy we have today is not a free economy. It is under the complete control of the ruling class (as opposed to being under the control of the

People of the United States and free markets).

Our economy at the end of WWII was regulated by a healthy balance of union labor, and industries that were appropriately taxed on war profits. In addition, America's competitors in the global market were in ruins from the war, and, most countries owed money to the United States because our Labor and manufacturers had provided huge amounts of logistical goods and equipment to allies during the war.

In that scenario, there was little need for a minimum wage because labor in the U.S. was in high demand, and, corporations operated for reasonable profits (paying reasonable taxes).

As America distanced itself from its wartime economy, the rules of economics changed. As more and more companies corrupted Congress and local governments, taxes were lowered on companies. Instead of using the extra tax-free profits to promote jobs in the U.S., those companies betrayed America and set up their business operations in other countries. In other countries, U.S. corporations could use an endless supply of workers, who were willing to work with no benefits, and work for $.027 per hour. U.S. companies used their profits, from tax breaks, to set up U.S. workers to compete with labor in other countries that was essentially slave labor.

This competition with slave labor, in other countries, was the beginning of the destruction of the middle class in the U.S. Coupled with Reagan's war on American workers, the use of slave labor in other countries guaranteed that Americans would suffer an accelerating decline in their standard of living. It also guaranteed that large multi-national business would drive smaller businesses into bankruptcy and remove millions of jobs from America and Americans.

What is "good for business" is no longer what is "good for America." What is "good for business," in terms of huge tax subsidies of multinational corporations, and, a severely depressed labor market in the U.S., is the beginning of the transition of the U.S. to a third-world economy. The fact is that "business" in the U.S. has a system that is rigged to force Americans to work harder, and harder, and harder, for less pay, while the "businesses" that own Congress make more, and more, and more money.

As Senator Sanders points out, for the past forty years, this rigged system has provided a huge transfer of wealth from the disappearing middle class to the few wealthy businesses and individuals at the top of the economic interests which have rigged the system.

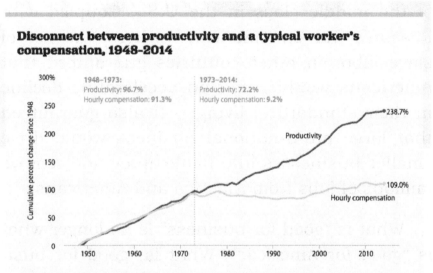

Disconnect between productivity and a typical worker's compensation, 1948-2014

1948–1973:
Productivity: 96.7%
Hourly compensation: 91.3%

1973–2014:
Productivity: 72.2%
Hourly compensation: 9.2%

Productivity 238.7%

Hourly compensation 109.0%

Note: Data are for average hourly compensation of production/nonsupervisory workers in the private sector and net productivity of the total economy. "Net productivity" is the growth of output of goods and services minus depreciation per hour worked.

Source: EPI analysis of data from the BEA and BLS (see technical appendix of *Understanding the Historic Divergence Between Productivity and a Typical Worker's Pay* for more detailed information)

There are at least ten good reasons to raise the minimum wage, over a period of a few years, to give minimum wage workers in the U.S. the same earning power they had in the 1960's.

First, we can appeal to the knowledge of seventy-five economists, 7 of whom are Nobel laureates, who convincingly tell us that raising the minimum wage (as it has been done many times in history) has little or no adverse effects on the economy. If anything, raising the minimum wage stimulates the economy, and, the resulting expansion in GDP more than pays for any of the minor disadvantages to raising the minimum wage.[24]

The second reason is that there is no basis for believing that raising the minimum wage causes a loss in jobs. The minimum wage has been raised many times, and although a very few businesses cannot handle the raise in wages, those businesses are soon replaced by new businesses. In addition, raising the minimum wage allows the ordinary people of the U.S. to spend more money on small businesses that are not large multinational corporations. Large multinational corporations tend to corrupt the government, abuse our infrastructure, and lower our living standards. Small businesses, on the other hand, create jobs, increase the quality of goods and services to the Nation, and, typically impose much less on the infrastructure and the

---

[24] *Seven Nobel Laureates Endorse Higher U.S. Minimum Wage*, Bloomberg Business, January 14, 2014.
http://www.bloomberg.com/news/articles/2014-01-14/seven-noble-laureates-urge-increase-in-u-s-worker-minimum-wage

ecology than large multinationals. The small businesses that spring up with an increase in minimum wages, as spending increases by ordinary people, create many more jobs than the few jobs that are lost when incompetent businesses (such as Walmart) go out of business. (Walmart is patently incompetent because it cannot pay livable wages to its employees. Such incompetent business should go out of business).

Third, it is only a myth that raising the minimum wage would destroy small businesses. In fact, 3 out of 5 small business owners are in favor of raising the minimum wage. Most minimum wage paying businesses are huge corporations that will do everything possible to avoid responsibly contributing to the economy in the U.S. Most large minimum wage paying companies, such as Walmart and McDonalds, have huge profits. They use their economic power to compete with small businesses. Small business must usually pay higher than minimum wage in order to attract workers. Raising the minimum wage forces large exploitative companies, such as Walmart and McDonalds to pay wages that are the same as small businesses pay. This gives small businesses more of an opportunity to compete with large multinationals that are a drain on our economy.

The fourth reason is that inflation is very much ahead of the minimum wage. If the minimum wage had kept pace with inflation indexes, it would be closer to $12.50 per hour. (Some credible estimates claim that it would be as high as $26.00 per hour for minimum wage workers to have the save standard of living they had in the 1960's).

The fifth reason is that saying we have "free markets" is a myth. Large moneyed interests have complete ownership of Congress, through Citizens' United, and there is endless legislation at the federal and state level to break unions and lower Americans' standard of living. The war on unions is actually a thinly disguised war on all workers in the U.S. and a war to artificially suppress wages for American workers. Trade agreements which promote the use of slave labor in other countries is a clear example of the relentless pressure, on our middle class, to relinquish fair wages and fair compensation for their labors.

Today, corporations spend roughly $2.6 billion each year lobbying Congress. That's why Republicans in Congress give tax breaks to billionaires, deny the reality of climate change and refuse to raise the minimum wage. **We need a Congress which represents working families, not just the top 1%.**

– Sen. Bernie Sanders (I-Vt.)

The sixth reason for raising the minimum wage is that low wages create a need for government subsidies. Contrary to media myths, most minimum wage workers are not entry-level workers. They are workers who are struggling just to survive and provide for the necessities of life. With minimum wages being less than livable wages, most minimum wage workers must have government subsidies to survive.

The seventh reason for raising the minimum wage is that it has the support of most religious organizations that declare a living wage takes precedence over profits. Although our populace disdains the very notion of morals, at present, some consider it appropriate to "do the right thing" and make certain that, in Senator Sanders words: "A job should elevate someone out of poverty, not keep them in it."

The eighth reason is that worker productivity justifies a raise in the minimum wage. If worker's wages kept pace with worker productivity in the U.S., the minimum wage would be $21.00 per hour. Businesses in the U.S. who are making record profits can afford to pay living wages.

The ninth reason is that 4.7 million working mothers, and 2.5 million working fathers would benefit from a living wage, as would their children. Without a raise in the living wage, increased taxes are necessary to assist those families living in poverty. Overall, a raise in the minimum wage would help remove 15 million workers from public assistance.

The tenth reason is the wide public support for raising the minimum wage. 75% of democrats and 53% of republicans support a raise in the minimum wage.

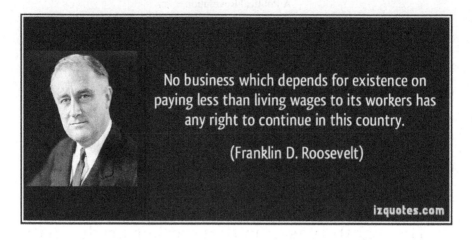

No business which depends for existence on paying less than living wages to its workers has any right to continue in this country.

(Franklin D. Roosevelt)

izquotes.com

Senator Sanders has been a leader in introducing legislation in Congress to raise the minimum wage to a morally and economically justified $15 per hour. He has introduced legislation in Congress to accomplish modest increase over a period of the next few years.

Senator Sanders' bill has the support of other members of Congress. It is most likely, however, that because of conservative opposition, a federal raise in the minimum wage is more likely to be passed, after the presidential election, as some form of economic reform package.

END THE WAR ON DRUGS

The so-called "war on drugs" is not really a war on drugs. It is s war on the People of the United States waged to justify a police state.

No social program in the U.S. has failed the American people more relentlessly than the "war on drugs" except for "prohibition."

Prohibition ended in 1933. The "war on drugs" began with the Johnson administration in 1965. It is amazing that the American people, and all of its institutions, could have failed to learn from the lessons of Prohibition, in so short of a time.

What Prohibition and the War on Drugs has shown us, over, and over, and over, again, is that trying to use laws, and law enforcement, to change peoples' abuse of substances is counterproductive.

The first thing that happens with a war on substances is that it immediately creates an incredible profit motive for organized crime to increase, not only the supply of the prohibited substance, but, also the use of the prohibited substance.

Time, after time, after time, throughout history, we should have learned that once organized crime has a profit motive, the profits they glean from trafficking in the prohibited substance soon work their way into the legitimate financial and economic infra-structure (through what is known as "money laundering").

The immense profits, and influence of the "drug wars" over the past forty years have concentrated enormous amounts of economic power into criminal organizations. Those organizations have laundered the money, using many devices from real estate investments to stock and commodity exchanges. The laundered proceeds are now showing up as substantial ownership, and controlling ownership of stock, in our publicly traded companies (often the stock is held by other companies, offshore, for the benefit of the criminal organizations).

The economic power of these organizations extends into our government itself. Some of the most corrupt criminal organizations in the U.S. are the police and law enforcement officers who are supposed to be protecting us from drug dealers. In reality, drug dealers have so much money from dealing in drugs that they can afford to bribe massive numbers of border agents, treasury agents, local police etc., to insure that only their competitors will ever be the target of law enforcement.

Many drug dealers have immunity from arrest and prosecution because they "cooperate" as confidential informants with police and the police will not arrest them. The result is that confidential informants create much of the street crime in the U.S. because they have special privileges with corrupt police. What is astonishing is that our corrupt and incompetent courts hardily approve of this corruption and facilitate it by protecting it. Courts are oblivious to the consequences of police mingling with criminals to "serve and protect."

In addition, with rulings such as the Citizens' United ruling, made by our Supreme Court, drug dealers are free to spend their profits, as much as they please, openly bribing any elected public official as much as they please. Criminals need only maintain an appearance of supporting a candidate, under the Citizens' United Ruling, in order to bribe the candidate with as much money as the criminal wants, in return for favors from the candidate.

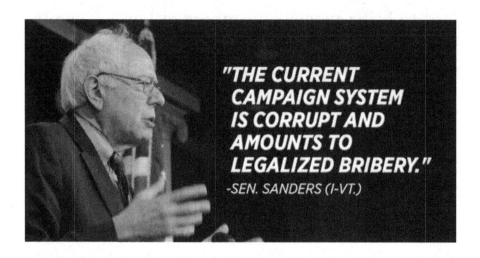

"THE CURRENT CAMPAIGN SYSTEM IS CORRUPT AND AMOUNTS TO LEGALIZED BRIBERY."

-SEN. SANDERS (I-VT.)

This results in a Congress, state and local governments, and a system of law enforcement, that is actually creating profits for drug dealers. Because "dirty money" can be easily used to corrupt our government, and law enforcement, our own governments are, directly or indirectly, protecting criminal organizations.

Rarely are the drug laws applied against large criminal organizations. Criminal narcotics organizations have the money to defend themselves in court, and, the money to pay experts to help them avoid detection and accountability. The war on drugs, therefore, was turned upon the "little people" in the U.S. The average person (especially poor people) has no chance against a criminal justice system that is backed by hundreds of billions of dollars, and, designed as a machine that insures convictions and guilty pleas. Because of the lack of due process rights, many, many people are forced to plead guilty, when they are actually innocent, simply because their conviction is assured by corrupt judges who provide "due process" only to law enforcement, and only to those who can pay for an expert legal defense, in the criminal justice process.

Consequently, our prisons are overflowing with small time drug users, most of who are minority men. This not only profits the narcotics organizations, by removing low level competitors from the streets, it also profits a huge private prison industry that is raking in Billions in profits each year. The private prison industry is one of the highest spending lobbying industries in the United States. Some private prison companies have go so far as to sue the government when their prisons are not full because prisons that are not full infringe on their profit making.

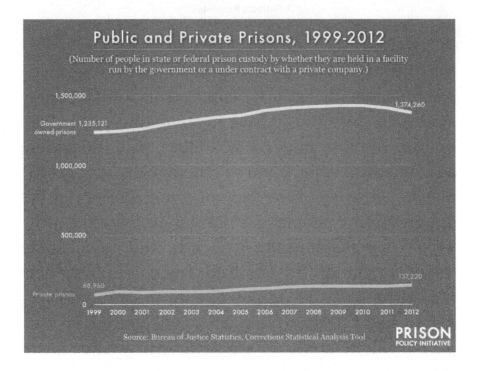

Needless to say, trial judges witlessly and happily feed the prison industry with a constant supply of ordinary citizens who, in most cases, have committed only minor crimes, or even no crimes at all.   This scenario gives trial judges the attitude that since they get their paychecks from the government, they must provide a constant stream of "convicted" citizens to the private prison industry, or, the source of their power and paycheck may be diminished along with the power of the state.

1 out of 4 male African-Americans born today will end up behind bars.

That is not the America we believe in.

BERNIESANDERS.COM

Judges, including the Supreme Court, consequently, have consciously slashed and gutted the U.S. Constitution and the Bill of Rights to the point where our Founders would not recognize them. The police in the United States are permitted to violate any individual rights they please with only occasional accountability. The judiciary has given them not only permission to violate individual rights, it has provided police with immunity for doing so.

These immunities, and police powers extended to law enforcement, by the judiciary, effectively place law enforcement above the law. Although the media occasionally reports police being held accountable for bribery, corruption and murder, these are merely atypical examples of police accountability. From no accountability, it became relatively easy for the militarized police forces in the U.S. to incarcerate some 2.5 million people – more than have ever been imprisoned in the history of the world. Most of these prisoners are minorities, and most of them are men.

Senator Sanders proposes substantial reforms to the criminal justice system. Among those reforms is the removal of harsh mandatory sentences, and, a reduction in the maximum sentences someone can receive for non-violent crimes. This would attenuate some of the power that law enforcement and the courts have to compel people to plead guilty.

The war on drugs, as a war on the People of the United States, must end.

Senator Sanders has recently introduced legislation in the Senate to eliminate private profit-motivated prisons in the next three years.

What is really needed to end the scourge of drugs in the U.S. is a plan to de-criminalize drugs, and, treat drug addiction as an illness. This plan must also be accompanied by revival of our middle class economy and job availability for addicts to re-enter society and avoid the societal forces that drive people to drugs as alternatives to gainful employment and a self-sustaining lifestyle. Our culture also needs to abandon its obsession with condemning and punishing people who are in many cases unable, without help, to extricate themselves from the darkness of drug addiction (including alcohol addiction).

Finally, we must have a realistic National health plan that addresses mental illness and substance abuse additions. Repeated studies show that drug addiction and drug problems are frequently a result of mental illness, and can best be addressed by a compassionate system of healthcare, rather than a massive prison-industrial complex and a corrupt system of courts.

REBUILD OUR CRUMBLING INFRASTRUCTURE

The infrastructure in the U.S. has been severely looted by the ruling elites. The immense tax subsidies and tax breaks provided to billionaires in the Reagan era, allowed Billionaires to reap enormous profits at the expense of the middle class, and, poorer Americans.

These tax breaks created revenue shortfalls for the United States. The ruling class now wants to cut the social safety net to make up for those shortfalls, while retaining the wealth that they skimmed from working Americans, and, America's infrastructure.

America is beginning to resemble a third world country. Our roads and bridges are degenerating. Our public transportation networks are based on technologies that are over a century old. Our telecommunications structure remains primitive because the telecommunications monopolies in this country refuse to upgrade communications. Telecommunications monopolies can make more profits manipulating consumers with oppressive contracts than they can make providing updated communications services. Our power generation system is little better than it was in the 19th Century as we continue to subsidize carbon emitting monopolies that suppress new technologies in power generation.

"For too many years, we've underfunded our nation's physical infrastructure. We have to change that and that's what the Rebuild America Act is all about. We must modernize our infrastructure and create millions of new jobs that will put people back to work and help the economy," Sanders said.

"My legislation puts 13 million people to work repairing the backlog of infrastructure projects all across this country. These projects require equipment, supplies and services, and the hard-earned salaries from these jobs will be spent in countless restaurants, shops and other local businesses. It's no surprise that groups across the political spectrum – from organized labor to the U.S. Chamber of Commerce – agree that investing in infrastructure will pay dividends for future generations." - Senator Bernie Sanders

Senator Sanders' proposals for re-building our infrastructure would be more likely to take hold if Senator Sanders and his supporters mandate the use of American made equipment in those infrastructure improvement projects. They are also more likely to take hold if we mandate that infrastructure improvement projects be awarded only to U.S. based firms, and, then only to U.S. based firms that create jobs for Americans.

American construction equipment is the finest in the world. Notwithstanding its tremendous value, American manufactured equipment is under assault in international trade. Countries such as China and Japan, ruthlessly devalue their currencies so as to preclude American made equipment from being exported overseas. The result is that we have huge trade imbalances with those countries. Because of currency manipulations (which are arguably against free trade agreements) Americans can afford American equipment, but other countries cannot afford that same equipment. This pattern of currency manipulation by other countries, to deny American manufacturers access to foreign markets, has been devastating to our manufacturers.

The result is that our annual trade deficits

are approaching over $600 Billion dollars per year. America desperately needs legislation that is going to protect American base businesses – businesses that do not outsource American jobs to other countries, and businesses that re-invest profits in American plants, American projects, and the creation of American jobs.

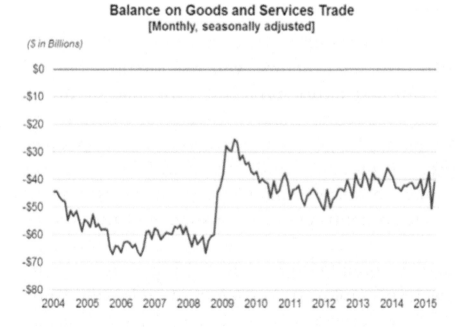

Figure 9 - Trade imbalance figures since the Bush Admin-istration, which shows the outrageous failure of Bush's eco-nomic policies. Source: U.S. Department of Commerce, Bu-reau of Economic Analysis.

Each of the $600 Billion dollars in trade imbalances, every year, is the equivalent of a transfer of America's wealth to other countries.

Senator Sanders' bills should provide trade restrictions that require the use of American made equipment, labor, materials and supplies in all infrastructure projects. This would be a legal and prudent check on the unscrupulous method of Pacific basin countries that seek to defeat American trade with currency manipulation.

Senator Sanders' legislative proposals should also favor contractors who use union labor on the infrastructure projects. The use of union labor frequently insures that a contractor will follow applicable laws. Unions act as an ever-present monitor, and check and balance, on contractors who might otherwise be willing to cheat on contracts at the expense of the American taxpayers. In addition, Unions strive to provide quality work. Requiring that all contractors employ union labor, in rebuilding our country, provides a level field for contractors competing for infrastructure projects. Otherwise, some contractors may be able to underbid projects, on the basis of using non-union labor, and secure those projects, but, ultimately turn out a poor quality project because they used cheap, unqualified labor instead of quality assured union labor.

Finally, we need effective regulations in our agencies that insure the interest of both American companies, and, American workers, are profoundly protected in the process of rebuilding our infrastructure. It is vital, in this political revolution, that Senator Sanders' supporters elect representatives in Congress who will insure that the interests of Americans, and American workers, are protected before protecting special interests.

RESTORE TAXES ON THE ONE PERCENT

Tax laws in the U.S. are currently designed to accomplish one thing, and one thing only. They are designed to transfer the wealth created in this country, to the wealthy, at the expense of the poor and the middle class.

This method of stealing from the middle class and the poor began in the Reagan era. At that time, only a few networks had full control over mass broadcast media in the U.S. Those media concerns used their grip on American audiences to persuade Americans of a variety of economic myths that still perpetuate to this day.

Myth #1: Give us the power to establish "law and order" and we will give you prosperity.

Myth #2: The best path to prosperity is to shower riches on the wealthy and those riches will be multiplied and "trickle down" to ordinary Americans.

Myth #3: Only the wealthy create jobs;

what's good for the wealthy is good for working Americans.

Myth #4: "Get government off our backs" means that getting "government off the backs" of the wealthy will get government off of the backs of working Americans.

Myth #5: Free trade agreements will allow us to "participate" in foreign economies and bring us wealth and jobs; flooding the U.S. with cheap, low quality foreign goods will (somehow) be good for working Americans.

In what stands in history as the single greatest war on the American worker, the Reagan regime declared war on labor unions, lowered wages nationwide, increased taxation on families and the middle class, exempted billionaires from taxes, created infinite loopholes and tax subsidies for multinational corporations, and permitted multinational corporations to use our infrastructure for a tiny fraction of the amount of tax money necessary to build or maintain it.

The result is the economy (and the depression) that we have today.

Figure 10 - Chart showing, accurately, what happened in the Reagan era that empowered the ruling class to steal infrastructure and labor value from the American working class.

In the Reagan era, the mass media in the U.S. was under the control of a small handful of networks. Those networks were, in turn, controlled by their multinational corporate sponsors. The result of this corporate propaganda scheme was that the ruling class convinced most Americans, that if taxpayers gave them huge tax discounted profits, they would use the extra money to create jobs.

The ruling class did create jobs. They created millions of jobs in China, Korea, Japan, Vietnam, Mexico, and other countries in which there were no labor laws, or organized labor. This resulted in the rise of exploiters, such as Walmart, flooding the United States, anticompetitively, with cheap goods that shut down over 60,000 manufacturers in the U.S.

Just since 2001 (the beginning of the Bush administration) 3.2 million American jobs were shut down in the U.S. and transferred to China alone.[25] To quote Senator Sanders – **"Enough is enough!"**

Theoretically, there were tax laws in place to prevent this abuse of the American economy. However, with billions to spend on legal fees and tax planners, lobbyists, and economic criminals, the ruling elite managed to make certain that loopholes in the tax law insured their profits would be almost tax free. They also insured that they would have no accountability for bankrupting the U.S. economy.

This scheme not only eliminated about 12

---

[25] *Outsource to China Cost U.S. 3.2 Million Jobs Since 2001*, U.S. News and World Report, December 11, 2014.

million manufacturing jobs from the United States, it also transferred about 30% of our wealth to the Pacific Basin. It is no wonder that weeks after President Reagan left office, the Japanese paid him $25 Million for a single speaking engagement. Reagan had almost singlehandedly insured that Japanese manufacturers would have no competition from U.S. manufacturers in U.S. markets.

Although most readers will not appreciate the details of the tax code, here is an example of how easily the ruling class uses the tax code to abuse Americans and the American economy.

One of the tax provisions the ruling class was able to obtain, during the Reagan administration, was a tax deferral on all of their profits that are outside the country. The profits would only be taxable if the ruling class brought the money back to the United States.[26] This provision insured that the ruling class would not use profits for the benefit of Americans, but, only for their own benefit in building overseas empires.

In 2001, several multinational corporations, by bribing Congressional legislators, passed a law that for one year would allow those large

---

[26] I.R.C. § 7701 (2015).

corporations to bring their profits to the U.S. for only 5% tax instead of the normal 35% tax.

Congress passed the tax revision, convincing Americans that money would flood back into the U.S. and create jobs. The multinationals brought back the money, paid the paltry 5% tax on it, and then, instead of using the money to create jobs in the U.S., they used the money to buy back their stock (making themselves even more wealthy than before). But this horror story didn't end there. To get the cash to pay for the buyback of their stock, they fired tens of thousands of U.S. workers. This was known as the era of "downsizing." The sole reason for it was greed. One company fired 40,000 workers after buying back their stock with offshore money taxed at the discount rate. Another company fired 60,000 workers.

American workers, and American taxpayers, paid the price.

Taxes on ordinary Americans, earning under $400,000 per year should remain at their current low rates.

This is one of the objectives of Senator Sanders if he is elected President. His objectives include his own tax strategies to establish taxes on heavy profit makers at pre-Reagan levels, (about 90% maximum) and, provide meaningful tax breaks for middle class and poor workers until the economy recovers. The funding of these tax breaks for the middle class and poor would also be funded by fair taxes on the offshore earnings of the companies that outsourced American jobs. It would also be paid by relatively small taxes on speculative market transactions.

Without these reforms, America will continue to transfer American jobs and American capital, to other countries, as opposed to encouraging our businesses to re-invest in America and Americans. Without these reforms, the death of the American middle class, and, the transition of the U.S. to a third world country, is assured.

Along with taxing offshore profits, as they currently exist, we need to start taxing companies that move jobs and operations to other countries. For example, Ford Motor Company, under a taxpayer bailout program, borrowed $9 Billion dollars from taxpayers in 2009. They used it to re-tool their equipment and manufacturing facilities. Ford has announced that it is building a new plant, not in the U.S., but in Mexico, at a cost of 2.5 Billion dollars. All of the jobs will go to Mexico, instead of to American workers, and American taxpayers are paying for this. Some people would call this "treachery."

We need a more effective, and, a more serious tax strategy to make companies which invest in other countries, responsible for paying what they use of American infra-structure, American defense, and American workers.

Our corporate controlled media in the U.S. conceals the fact that the wealthy 1% in the U.S., and, U.S. multinational corporations, consume the largest share of our nation's infrastructure. At the same time, the wealthy and the multinational corporations pay the lowest percentage of taxes to reimburse the American People for their use of our infrastructure.

Conservative demagogues are fond of pointing out that corporate tax rates are the highest in the industrialized world at 35% of earnings. What these demagogues conceal, however, is that American corporations have, literally, thousands of loopholes that enable them to avoid most of their income ever being subject to the 35% tax rate.

In addition, corporate shareholders in the

U.S. are able to avoid responsible taxation on their earnings because they are taxed at a favorable "capital gains rate" which is about one half of what the ordinary American is required to pay on their earnings.

We must being taxing overseas profits.

Piling Up

Foreign profits of major U.S. firms have been accumulating offshore as companies reinvest them overseas and defer U.S. tax.

Total foreign indefinitely reinvested earnings (IRE)

2013 **$2.119 trillion**

Top companies with IRE balances in 2013, in billions

General Electric	$110.0
Microsoft	$76.4
Pfizer	$69.0
Merck	$57.1
Apple	$54.4
IBM	$52.3
Johnson & Johnson	$50.9
Cisco Systems	$48.0
Exxon Mobil	$47.0
Citigroup	$43.8

Source: Audit Analytics

The Wall Street Journal

Figure 11 - Wall Street Journal estimates of companies who are evading taxes on profits by refusing to repatriate the profits they obtained from moving American jobs overseas.

REDUCE THE ENDLESS MILITARY SPENDING

Polls across the world show that the majority of the world's population considers the United States to be the most significant threat to
peace on the planet.

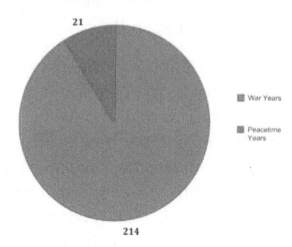

Calendar Years the U.S. Has Been At
War Since 1776

Military spending now accounts for 60% per

year of America's discretionary budget.

Senator Sanders, and his supporters, consistently acknowledge the important role that the Military plays in our national security. They also deeply appreciate the contributions of veterans to America.

On the other hand, Senator Sanders also recognizes that war should be the last resort to the resolution of world issues. In his views, the costs and horrors of war should not be imposed on the U.S., or the world, if it is possible to avoid war through diplomacy or other means.

Senator Sanders has also brought to the public's attention that the Department of Defense is, literally, not able to account for almost 2.1 Trillion dollars in spending.

As President, Senator Sanders would have complete discretion, as commander in chief, over the military's budget. As a matter of checks and balances, he has hinted that his strategy would be to use the General Accounting Office to first straighten out the defense budget. Unfortunately, the GAO has reported to the current administration that the Department of Defense records are so poor that it is not able to audit the Department as it would audit other agencies. An audit of astronomical defense spending may not be feasible. We may need extensive new laws, from Congress, to control "out-of-control" defense spending.

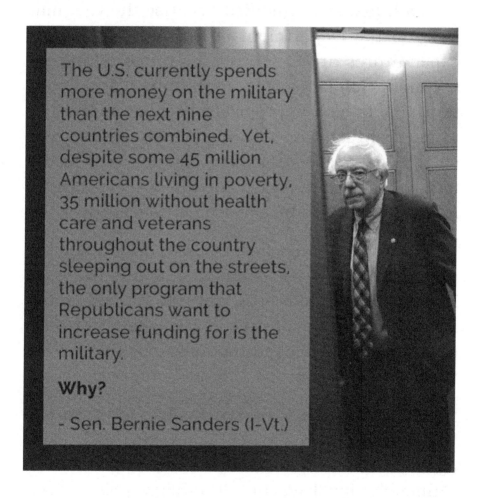

The U.S. currently spends more money on the military than the next nine countries combined. Yet, despite some 45 million Americans living in poverty, 35 million without health care and veterans throughout the country sleeping out on the streets, the only program that Republicans want to increase funding for is the military.

Why?

- Sen. Bernie Sanders (I-Vt.)

In addition to controlling defense spending as a means of reducing tax burdens on ordinary

Americans, Senator Sanders has proposed a "war tax." This would be levied on industries, and individuals, that specifically profited from the second Iraq war, and, the ones that profit from any wars in the future.

Such taxes are justified because the vast majority of the Department of Defense's enormous expenditures are to protect the property and investments of large U.S. multinational corporations. It is also appropriate because most U.S. arms manufacturers receive huge government subsidies. These subsidies come not only in the form of tax deductions, but also in the form of indirect subsidies by government agencies.

The Ex/Im bank, for example, finances many of the weapons packages that giants such as Boeing, Martin Marietta, and McDonnell Douglas sell to other countries. These giants also receive huge subsidies in the form of services from various agencies in the U.S. government.

Many Americans do not realize, for example, that the Department of Commerce is a sub agency of the Department of State and that it is intimately involved in all foreign policy decisions, especially those pertaining to going to war. The Department of State and the Department of Commerce are incredibly expensive agencies that mostly benefit multinational oil corporations, and, multinational weapons manufacturers.

This massive "military industrial complex" needs to start paying its own way. Through carefully controlled "national security" scares, and, bombarding Americans with "national security" propaganda, this military industrial complex has been able to frighten U.S. taxpayers into paying the wealthy owners of war industries for the last half of a century. It is time that the military industrial complex start paying its own way, instead of using scare tactics to extort money from average Americans.

One thing seems certain. Senator Sanders' track record in Congress proves that his administration would be far less susceptible to false information, that is disseminated by the corporate controlled mass media, designed to inflate military spending. Senator Sanders was one of the few members of Congress to vote against the Bush regime's war in Iraq. Senator Sanders was one of the few who was not fooled by the deceptive propaganda from the ruling elite.

"Enough is enough."

EXPAND SOCIAL SECURITY

Social Security is a part of our safety net, and, it is preventing our economy from completely collapsing.

Contrary to ruling class propaganda, the social security system is not an "entitlement" program. The social security system is a government-supervised system of private savings. Any person who receives social security benefits has paid into the system for many years.

Notwithstanding the fact that benefits from the social security system are private property, mainstream media in the U.S. has begun a propaganda campaign to take it away from Americans. That propaganda seeks to convince younger voters that Social Security is a tax burden on younger voters. That same propaganda seeks to portray the Social Security system as "broke" because it is another failed "social program."

In truth, the social security system is not broke. To fund improvident wars, Congress has repeatedly borrowed from social security. The money the United States is required to pay back the social security fund is a debt, not a social program. The money that working Americans pay into social security is held in a "trust fund" that is supposed to keep it safe for us. Unfortunately, as the "trust fund" is completely controlled by politicians and bureaucrats, it is far from safe.

Bush created the war in Iraq. He did not have Congressional funding for it. Consequently, he "borrowed" the money from the Social Security trust fund to wage war. The only thing the trust fund received, in return, were IOU's from the U.S. Treasury. Because of interest rate manipulation, those IOU's carry very little interest. The interest rate on those IOU's is about 1/3 of what is necessary to keep pace with inflation.

Now, conservatives are claiming that the social security "trust fund" is going bankrupt. They want to cut social security benefits (benefits which are private property of American Citizens) so that they can "balance the budget." Part of their plan to "balance the budget" is to try to not re-pay the IOU's until inflation has reduced the debt on those IOU's to a relatively small amount. The IOU's to the Social Security trust fund are scheduled to come due in 2020.

Rather than cut social security, and privatize the social security system, Senator Sanders seeks to expand social security.

There are some laws in the way of that expansion.

Under current laws, billionaires are exempt from paying social security taxes on their income to the extent that their income exceeds about $250,000.

Social Security is NOT going broke.

Social Security has a surplus of $2.76 trillion and can pay out benefits to all eligible Americans until 2033.

Passing legislation that I wrote, which would lift the cap on taxable income above $250,000, would extend Social Security solvency for 47 years. And that is exactly what we must do!

- Sen. Bernie Sanders (I-Vt.)

If this one impediment to fair taxation is removed, then, the social security fund will be secure for, effectively, an indefinite period of time.

To really insure the stability and safety of social security, and the social security fund, perhaps the future will hold legislation that requires all government employees, and Congress, to equally participate in social security as is required of all Americans. This would vastly increase the stability of the program, and, would likely increase the protection of the program, over long periods of time, as political interests might hesitate before attempting to dismantle it.

Perhaps Senator Sanders' plans for the expansion of social security is to create a uniform system of social safety nets, under the Social Security system, that would return a modest standard of living for disabled and elderly people in the U.S. Such a system is in place in a number of European countries. Such a system serves the People without adding to the costs of doing business, and, thankfully was in place to prevent the starvation of many People after the Bush depression of 2008.

DEMILITARIZE THE POLICE
END POLICE BRUTALITY

Demilitarizing the police and ending police brutality are two sides of the same coin. Senator Sanders points out that police brutality is a symptom of many social ills in America such as racism, institutional racism, a failed criminal justice system, poverty, lack of mental health programs, and a profit driven system of private prisons. However, the militarization of our police force, nationwide, is also a huge factor that is driving police brutality, torture, police murders of civilians, and a large number of social ills.

Many people do not realize that when people applaud police brutality, and, step up police brutality in one location, it tends to send criminal elements to other locations. Consequently, the more cities and towns spend on law enforcement, the more they are likely to drive crime to other cities and towns. Those cities and towns then need to spend huge sums on escalating their police forces to commit brutality on criminals that have come there from other cities and towns that spent more than they did for police "protection." This leads into a spiraling competition between cities and towns to out-spend each other on police so that they drive "undesirables" to each other by spending on police. In effect, cities and towns must spend money on police to protect themselves from the criminals who flee cities and towns that spend a lot of money on police.

Ultimately, "undesirables" end up accumulating in poor and impoverished cities and towns who cannot afford to spend too much on police. In those towns, the police often turn to brutality as a means of controlling the "undesirables." In those impoverished towns and cities, the "undesirables then become the focus of "law and order" fanaticism. This fanaticism has resulted in the following:

> A private prison industry that is the largest lobbyist in the U.S., and, which imprisons the largest number of people in the history of humanity.

➤ Corrupt and incompetent judges who are dedicated to convicting people at all costs.

➤ A corporate media that glorifies police brutality and police murder of Americans.

➤ An obsessive "Dirty Harry" mindset that pervades our culture through endless repetition in popular media.

➤ The rise of fascism in governments in the U.S.

➤ The "war on drugs" that actually increases the use and supply of drugs, and, enriches criminal enterprises.

➤ Judicial destruction of the U.S. Constitution and State Constitutions.

➤ "Guilty until proven innocent" standards which justify brutality and obliterates compassion.

➤ Criminalization of mental illness.

➤ Poverty and joblessness, and,

> Massive burdens on taxpayers for sustaining a spiteful and dysfunctional "criminal justice" system.

Almost all of Senator Sanders' social programs will, directly or indirectly have a positive influence on the problem of police brutality and police militarization. However, even if all of Senator Sanders' social programs become law, are fully funded, and, fairly implemented, it will not solve the problem of police brutality without some strong legislation aimed at police misconduct and de-militarizing the police.

We need to vastly expand our enlightenment, as a civilization, on the implementation of violence by police as a solution to social problems.

Senator Sanders is fond of saying that he was a mayor of Burlington, Vermont and that he knows that the police have a "difficult job." With all respect to Senator Sanders, all Americans have "difficult jobs." It is not an excuse for using deadly force. One of the most common excuses for police violence against the People is that the police face danger.

This excuse is hammered into the minds of Americans through countless television programs, and movies, that glorify the police as heroes who are beyond question or reproach.

Certainly, police can become heroes as any other professional, or any American, can be a hero. Most Americans do something heroic in their lifetime. However, in terms of facing death or injury on the job, police are not even in the top 10 of dangerous jobs in the U.S. We do not need to empower them to murder and maim, at will, in the name of "officer safety."

Police are more likely to die from heart attacks while on the job, and, from failing to wear their seatbelts on the job, than they are to die from citizen violence.

Police are three times more likely to be shot by another policeman than they are likely to be shot by a citizen.

Our current problem is compounded by incompetent judges who have licensed police to escalate violence, at any time against citizens, and then apply deadly force as the officer becomes "afraid" of the violence that arose from his escalation of the situation.

This sense of entitlement for police to use

violence began in the 1970's with the advent of the "Dirty Harry" mentality. "Dirty Harry" knew everything. He appointed himself as police, judge and executioner of anyone he felt was "breaking the law." The immensely popular movie, and the immense popularity of the character "Dirty Harry" (played by Clint Eastwood) led to four decades of mass media glorifying the police to the point that they are a worshipped class and above the law.

On the heels of this brainwashing, entire industries arose in the U.S., including the private prison industry, that support and drive the perpetuation of justifications for police brutality, and, a militarized police force.

Judges have almost completely abandoned due process and fairness in criminal trials in favor of supporting the popular "law and order," or "Dirty Harry" mentality.

The result is a "criminal justice" system in which judges, the final guardians of due process, act as nothing more than rubber stamps of approval for police and police misconduct. This "Dirty Harry" mentality is a "stone-age" concept and needs to be re-evaluated and re-addressed.

In addition, a huge proliferation of both federal and state laws, that gave prosecutors almost complete control over criminal trials, resulted in a system in which an accused person is automatically guilty. The only way to overcome this perception and presumption of guilt in our legal system is to spend huge sums of money for investigators, and, influential law firms, to obtain a fair trial. Those accused relegated to public defenders face the realities of judges hostile to "due process" arguments, and, public defenders who are unfairly burdened with huge numbers of cases. (In all fairness, public defenders are frequently very well trained and are very capable trial lawyers; however, their workloads usually vastly exceed those of the combined prosecutor/police teams who are funded at many times the level of the public defenders).

Police are required to have no more evidence in making an arrest than a mere suspicion. Prosecutors are required to have nothing more than police reports (even if the reports are completely false or exaggerated) in order to file charges. The result is that many people (especially minorities) are charged with crimes even when there is little chance of conviction in a **fair** trial. They are imprisoned before any opportunity for trial. Harsh pre-trial conditions are often imposed on their release prior to trial. Then, during the pre-trial process, they are often railroaded (jail without affordable bail can be so demeaning and despairing that many plead guilty just to "get it over with") into pleading guilty to crimes that they have not committed. Laws that provide outrageously long sentences for even minor infractions of the law, such as possession of small amounts of marijuana, force the innocent to plead guilty, in exchange for a guaranteed lighter sentence, rather than risk a trial custom tailored by a corrupt judge to insure the prosecution's success. Many defendants are properly counseled that their best alternative is to plead guilty, rather than go to trial and face immense sentences tainted by a police state judge.

Senator Sanders has not yet proposed direct legislation to control police brutality and diminish the militarization of our 1,247,000 police.

Senator Sanders acknowledges, in public appearances, that police must be held accountable when they do something wrong. He has also acknowledged that there must be specific "rules" for the use of deadly force so that the police are held accountable for murders.

Unfortunately, history has shown us that both the police, and corrupt judges, have no qualms about ignoring laws. Even if the President and Congress were to pass proper laws protecting Americans from the police, judges may very well ignore those laws, or find intellectually corrupt ways of avoiding them.

We must demilitarize our police forces so they don't look and act like invading armies.

Bernie

We need a serious and independent system of holding police accountable for brutality. We need a serious system that does not permit police to break laws, any laws, in the pursuit of criminals. We need a system of mandating accountability for police who employ force, or deadly force, in the context of police operations.

One way to accomplish this is to mandate that any law enforcement agency must have private insurance, against which a victim of police brutality may make a claim. It is likely that insurance companies would make an excellent effort, with premium incentives, to keep violent police out of government. If an officer repeatedly uses unnecessary force, and the insurance company is compelled to pay for it, the insurance company, through its right of private contract with the law enforcement agency, will be able to force "bad cops" out of law enforcement.

Victims should have recourse to enforce their claims against police in special courts. These courts would automatically provide a jury trial for the claimants, and, would be presided over by judges who have no connections to the state, the police, or the insurance companies which are required to pay on police brutality claims.

We should also vastly reduce the number of law enforcement personnel in the United States. Our very own Constitution is designed to prevent the police state that now exists in America.

Finally, we need to reduce the arms that police are entitled to employ in day to day contacts with ordinary citizens. This should include uniforms and appearances that are more conducive to police "protecting and serving" the public instead of brutalizing the public. We also need to change the self-image of police from that of untouchable heroes to one that recognizes their fallibility and their need to be polite and respectful to citizens. Finally, we need strict laws to punish police who escalate encounters with citizens into violent situations.

If Senator Sanders and his supporters truly wish to achieve fair police accountability, and, demilitarize America's occupying police force, there will also have to be accountability and consequences, for corrupt and incompetent judges, who disregard laws designed to protect the People against a police state that is out of control.

We need rules and laws that will direct the police against economic and financial criminals on Wall Street instead of over a million police

obsessed with imprisoning citizens on petty
charges.

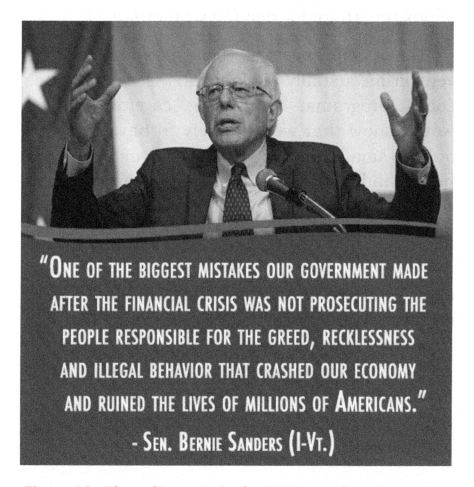

"ONE OF THE BIGGEST MISTAKES OUR GOVERNMENT MADE
AFTER THE FINANCIAL CRISIS WAS NOT PROSECUTING THE
PEOPLE RESPONSIBLE FOR THE GREED, RECKLESSNESS
AND ILLEGAL BEHAVIOR THAT CRASHED OUR ECONOMY
AND RUINED THE LIVES OF MILLIONS OF AMERICANS."

- SEN. BERNIE SANDERS (I-VT.)

Figure 12 - The police state in the U.S. is not there to protect
us from the "bad guys;" It is there to protect the "bad guys"
from us.

Finally, we need social programs that allevi-
ate the root causes of crime. We need a com-

prehensive system of mental health treatment. We need to create jobs, and positive incentives for those who we have discarded into prisons and ghettos. We need to employ compassion, as opposed to only spite and punishment, as part of our repertoire for dealing with crime.

Those who object to social programs to prevent crime usually exclaim at the cost of such social programs. However, careful analysis would show that we are likely to have to spend only a small fraction of the cost of a massive prison industrial complex, and massive militarized police forces, to achieve positive results through alternative social programs.

Arguably, the immense greed of the ruling class in America has been responsible for most of the social ills now driving crime. We can eliminate many of the causes of crime in the U.S., by restraining the ruling class that is causing it, and, demilitarizing the invading army that the ruling class has convened against our own people.

EPILOGUE
"COMES THE TIME ... COMES THE MAN"

Senator Sanders has sparked a groundswell of enlightened Americans who see through the charade, and deceit, of corporate media and corrupt politicians in the American system of government.

The political revolution of Senator Sanders is one that, above all, originates with the People of the United States.

When elected, Senator Sanders will continue to need the unified support of all of his followers. Senator Sanders' revolution will require that the People register to vote, and, most importantly, get out and vote. This pattern of activism must continue after Senator Sanders is elected. We, the People, must vote out incumbents who have track records of supporting their wealthy and influential donors, instead of supporting the hundreds of millions of ordinary Americans they were supposed to serve.

From the Presidency, Senator Sanders would have two powerful tools for reforming our corrupt political system. First he will have veto power.

Our system is designed so that (with the exception of our corrupt judicial system) all branches of government must give their consent before something becomes the "law of the land." As President, Senator Sanders would have the veto power of the presidency to use to negotiate the passage of laws that are in favor of the People, instead of moneyed special interests. If Congress continues its relentless pattern of passing laws that only benefit the ruling elite, instead of benefitting the People, Senator Sanders, hopefully, will have the resolve to use the veto power of the presidency to force special interests to consider the People's agenda. Senator Sanders could use the President's veto authority to veto opposition legislation until, and unless, it includes balancing provisions that are in the interests of ordinary Americans. Hopefully, Senator Sanders, as President, would compel Congress to pass laws that are friendly to workers, families, individuals, and those of us who seek to restore the individual liberties of which we have been stripped in the past forty years.

The second tool that Senator Sanders will

have as President is his use of the Whitehouse as a "bully pulpit" for the People. Senator Sanders has proven his ability to mobilize the People. As President, he will have the visibility and political power to alert the People to those machinations of government that further threaten the health and welfare of this great nation. With continued mobilization of voters, and with Senator Sanders' guidance, We the People can reclaim our country, and the American dream from the ruling class that seeks to destroy it for their own gain and profit.

Many pundits and commentators have asked how Senator Sanders has risen so quickly in the eyes of the public as the best candidate to lead our great Nation.

Perhaps it is because Senator Sanders is an idealist, just like our Founders. He is a man who has a unique vision honoring this great country, and, the American People. His idealism is tempered with his sagacious experience as a career leader, showing a career spanning decades in the service of the People who elected him, and, entrusted their governance to his integrity, courage and commitment.

"Comes the Time, Comes the Man"

"St. Thomas More" –Shakespeare

"Feel the Bern."

ABOUT THE AUTHOR

John Davis (1953 -) was born in Cleveland, Ohio. He was educated at Case Western Reserve University (BA) (one of the top ten universities in the United States), Seattle University School of Law (JD), and, New York University School of Law (LL.M post-doctoral) (one of the top ten law schools in the United States). John is fluent in seven languages (including ancient Latin and Greek). He has travelled the world over, many times, and has represented clients, in his thirty-five year career, such as the United States Government and the Federation of Russia.

He has been a prosecutor three times in his 35-year career. He has held positions such as

Assistant Attorney General, United States Speaker, and Deputy District Attorney.

For most of his career in civil law, John was a successful international lawyer, practicing in many nations around the world.

John is now retired.

Made in the USA
Las Vegas, NV
04 December 2024

13346591R00144